P.R.I.D.E

Practical Guide Leading To Success
In Professional Career and Life

By Sandeep Agarwal

STARDOM BOOKS

STARDOM BOOKS

WORLDWIDE

www.StardomBooks.com

STARDOM BOOKS

A Division of Stardom Publishing

and infoYOGIS Technologies.

105-501 Silverside Road

Wilmington, DE 19809

FIRST EDITION OCTOBER 2018

Stardom Books

P.R.I.D.E

Practical Guide Leading to Success
in Professional Career and LIFE.

Sandeep Agarwal

p. cm.

Category: Self-Help/Career

ISBN-13: 978-1-7323287-4-7

ISBN-10: 1-7323287-4-9

DEDICATION

To my parents, wife, and kids,
You mean the world to me. This book is dedicated to all
those who came into my life, enriched and helped me build a
purpose, taught me important lessons, and guided me.

WHEN YOU CAME IN THIS WORLD,
YOU CRIED, and the WORLD SMILED.
LIVE YOUR LIFE SUCH THAT
WHEN YOU LEAVE THIS WORLD,
YOU SMILE, and the WORLD CRIES

– Sant Kabir Das

ABOUT THE AUTHOR

Sandeep Agarwal has 25+ years of industry experience covering a broad portfolio in across diverse sectors such as Industrial, Consumer Electronics, Digital Enterprise, Telecom Communications, Enterprise Networking, Embedded Technologies and Data Center Domains.

At Happiest Minds, Sandeep built the ER&D business acquiring some major and marque customers in Networking, Industrial, Semi and Embedded Technologies.

Sandeep helped incubate the IoT focus and forged solid partnerships with MNCs and many other companies to provide end-to-end solutions and system integration services to Happiest Minds' customers.

As part of the Senior Leadership Team, Sandeep supports various major and minor initiatives at the company level. Sandeep also actively participates in the ER&D council at IESA and NASSCOM apart from actively participating in the start-up eco-system.

Prior to joining Happiest Minds, Sandeep was with MindTree for 12+ years and was part of the core team that was instrumental in growing MindTree's Product Engineering Services business in the global market. He played a key role in establishing successful multi-year relationships with a host of Fortune500 companies. Sandeep was also a recipient of MindTree's prestigious Chairman's award and Citizen's award and headed the PM Council at MindTree for the year 2007-2008.

Sandeep started his career with Tata Unisys in Mumbai, and then moved onto working with Lucent Technologies Bell labs as part of their 3GPP/UMTS initiatives in the late nineties.

Sandeep is a regular speaker at international and domestic industry events and he is a core member of Words of Peace, Global non-profit organization to support and spread message of peace promoted by its founder Mr. Prem Rawat.

ACKNOWLEDGEMENTS

The book is an acknowledgement to my parents Mr. Babulal Agarwal and Mrs. Shakuntala Agarwal and my living master Mr. Prem Rawat, whose teachings have impacted all aspects of my life since my childhood days. I would like to express my gratitude to my wife Vandana, kids Tanish and Riti and sister Ujwala Modi, brothers Hemant and Manoj who have blessed and supported me making me who I am today.

On the professional front, gratitude goes out to my role model Mr. Ashok Soota, Mr. Subroto Bagchi, Mr. Janakiraman, and many other friends and colleagues who have supported me throughout this journey. My learnings are attributed to their timely and precious guidance.

I have taken short stories from the internet; the intention was to accentuate a particular point and provide the reader with clarity on the respective topic. All credit belongs to respective authors; the use of these stories has helped me complete the framework and drive the point of 'Designing your personal and professional LIFE.'

Last but not the least, I would like to thank my publisher and good friend Mr. Raam because of whom I am able to put my life learnings into this book and share it with you. I hope you find this useful and encouraging to build a LIFE you genuinely desire and helping you towards being successful.

TABLE OF CONTENT

FOREWORD

Most corporate executives are familiar with the need to have mission, vision and values statements for the organization. Sandeep Agarwal has adapted this approach for individuals and through his book, P.R.I.D.E. has created an invaluable tool for young professionals to plan their careers and lives successfully.

P.R.I.D.E. is written in a flowing, easy to read style and the lessons supported by anecdotes, examples and personal experience. Sandeep continuously raises questions which individuals must ask to understand themselves better. If I had to pick one anecdote as my favourite, it is about the king and his four wives; the punch lines at the end have a lesson for all of us.

Having known Sandeep for well over a decade, I would say that he lives by the values he endorses in P.R.I.D.E. which accounts for the sincerity that shines through his book.

Ashok Soota

Executive Chairman, Happiest Minds Technologies Pvt Ltd
Co-Author: Entrepreneurship Simplified: From Idea to IPO

PREFACE

THE CHALLENGES FACED BY YOUNG PROFESSIONALS

The vast majority of young people today are living in developing countries. According to the United Nations, globally, around 85 percent of 15 to 23 years-old's live in developing countries, a figure projected to grow to 89.5 per cent by 2025. Among them, some live in rural areas but many inhabit the overpopulated metropolitan areas of India, Mongolia and other parts of Asia.

Young lives in the developing countries are defined by poverty, famine, lack of sanitation and clean water. Health problems are rife, especially due to the prevalence of lifestyle diseases in certain regions. The UN estimates that 200 million young people live in poverty, 130 million are illiterate and 10 million live with lifestyle diseases.

Youth is the foundation of a future revolution, the owners of tomorrow who carry the zeal to create a new world. We must take responsibility of the coming generations and position them in a manner that they can create a sustainable future for themselves.

The question is - How do we empower them?

As young professionals step into a corporate world or start their businesses, they are at a unique point in their life. These are the young folks in their early twenties, wanting to enter a professional world from their academic world.

A dreamer, enthusiast, full of life and ready to enter the professional world.

Young professionals desire to achieve a lot, be successful, stand on their own feet, earn their own money, create their own identity. As the days and months pass, they start getting lost in their daily routine, not knowing:

Why are they doing, what they are doing?

In the absence of this simple foundation of life, the Why, the What, and the How, they start taking things very lightly, getting into a comfort zone, and start losing some of the very crucial years of their years which would have helped them create a foundation. There are many self-help books and a lot of information available on the internet, but this book attempts to simplify the basics and provide them with a framework that would help the young generation create an ultimate purpose in their life and live a life they truly want or desire.

Though the book is meant for young professionals, this could be used at any stage of your professional career, as many people can relate to these even at a later stage, while going through a mid-life crisis.

This book aims to create a simple and strong foundation starting from:

- Identifying the life purpose – the why?
- Defining the vision – the what?
  and
- Creating the professional values – the how?

In my 25 years of experience, I have learned a lot of lessons, many by experiences, some by mistakes, some through my good friends, and some from unknown people who entered my life and taught me a valuable lesson.

The book is aimed at putting all this together into a well-defined framework. This framework can help you create your own customized and personalized purpose-filled life, and help build the life and path you truly want.

PART ONE: NEED FOR KNOWING YOUR PURPOSE AND DEFINING YOUR VISION & VALUES

You were born, and you came to this world. Now you are here, and one day you will be gone.

- What do you want to leave behind as a legacy?
- What should you be known for when you leave this world?
- What should you be remembered for?

Your achievements, your attitude, your simplicity, your love, your support, your kindness, your humbleness, or what?

It is important to understand WHY you want to do, what you want to do?

It is not easy to know the why. This book is a practical guide, providing you with ways to understand yourself and your true passion or desires. This will help you design and build your own life.

Once you identify your purpose (the why?), you can start defining your vision towards the same (the what?). The Why and What are essential foundation blocks. Once you have defined those, you will really start following some life values that will guide your behavior, drive you towards your goals, and shape you towards leading a very successful and happy life.

Identify your life purpose – the Why?

There is a purpose for everything we do. Right?

For studying, for working, for driving, for marriage, for business, for creating an organization, or for some projects or tasks you do on a daily basis. All this is part of the activities or actions you do in life.

So if everything you do in your life is for some purpose, isn't it essential to identify your own life's purpose?

The purpose of your existence, the things you want to be remembered for?

The dictionary defines purpose as "the reason why something is done or created or for which something exists." For example, you are conducting a meeting to solve a problem at hand possibly.

One such example of identifying a life purpose is "Making an Impact to a Million Lives" – This purpose though simple it may sound, has a profound meaning that would change how you do things, your behavior and actions. You would start finding ways or defining goals where you start impacting the lives of people for good with your actions. We will go into more details of identifying your life purpose in Chapter 1.

Define your vision – the What?

Once we have identified the life purpose, we have a goalpost set for life. The next question would be, what goals would you take to achieve your purpose? There are long-term goals and short-term goals. Short-term goals are baby steps taken to achieve your long-term goals.

Defining the vision is an important step, as that will articulate clearly what goals and measurable criteria you want to achieve. The vision is set using the SMART acronym that stands for:

- Specific - being very specific in defining your goals
- Measurable - goals that can be easily measurable
- Achievable – goals that are not impossible
- Relevant – goals that are relevant to your purpose
- Time-Bound – goals that have specified target timelines to achieve.

The relevance part will drive the focus to the purpose, and the others will keep your goals in the right direction defined against a timeline which will help you track the progress towards achievement. Once the goals are defined, it will be easy to achieve them and check on the progress that you are making.

Examples of defining specific Vision/GOAL could be

- Be the CEO of the company by the time you have 25 years of experience.
- Create a business and grow the business by 10x in the next five years.
- Achieve a financial goal of saving $1 Million in the next five years.
- Providing education to 100,000 kids and helping them get to a career track by 2025.

We will look into more details about defining your vision/goal in Chapter 2.

Living with your values– the how?

Your values guide and direct your behavior. Values are principles or standards that define a behavior; it is one's judgment to decide what is important in your life. The values are guiding principles which will help you keep yourself on track and achieve your goals and finally, achieve your life's purpose.

I was lucky enough to work in two of the most valued organizations, MindTree for 12.5 years and HappiestMinds for 6 years now. The value system in these two organization inculcates a culture to work in a team and some basic code of conduct that would drive the commonality while working with the teams.

In part two of this book, I will take you through my learnings and define certain principles and standards that will help you make your professional life successful. I have used an acronym P.R.I.D.E which stands for Professionalism, Responsibility, Integrity, Development, and Excellence. The implementation of this acronym would ultimately drive you towards your purpose, and help achieve the goals you have set along the way. The definition of P.R.I.D.E and how you can bring a PRIDE moment to yourself are more detailed in part two of this book.

1

IDENTIFY YOUR LIFE PURPOSE – THE WHY?

The Two Most Important Days In Your Life Are The Days You Were Born And The Day You Find Out Why? - Mark Twain.

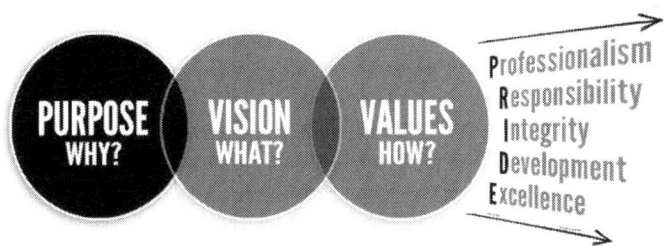

You are often caught between:

what you want to do,

vs

what do others want from you?

vs

what your skills are for which you will get paid for?

The day you can align all of this, meaning what you want to do aligns with your profession, and that aligns with what you get paid for that, you are aligned with the true purpose of your life. Many times this is not true. You do something because of certain factors like your salaried job, your family business, your expectations from family and friends and many other stated and unstated needs. You are so caught up in day-to-day work that you miss the whole purpose. Life starts dragging you and especially in a professional career knowingly or unknowingly you get caught up in the rat race.

Hence, it is essential to keep looking inside, introspecting, spending time with yourself, to remove the weight from your shoulders and to start reflecting on what you exactly want in life.

Passion is something that you love doing most, it is something that many people are unaware of, and it's not simple to find the real passion and hence the true purpose of your life.

Below are specific ways that may help you find yourself and the real passion within you, which would then guide you to your true purpose.

Reflect on things that you love doing:

Start making notes on what you love doing. Even during the course of your daily job, write down the actions or work that you enjoyed doing,

- Was it cracking a problem?
- Was it helping others?
- Was it winning a big project?
- Was it making an impact on society as a whole?
- Was it a big challenge you solved?
- Was it the support you provided which made a difference to someone's life?

These are good indications to start analyzing what you like and love to do. Analyzing this queries, and finding the answers to this will direct you to start identifying your life's purpose.

Introspect

Take time out to introspect and reflect on what you would like to become, try and answer this questions:

- What should I be known for when I die?
- What should people remember me for?
- If I die tomorrow, what legacy am I living behind?
- How will people remember me when I am not in this world?
- What are the interferences that are holding me back?
- What makes me happy?
- What desirable roles resonate with me?
- If I am reading books or watching movies, what are the parts I truly loved?
- What are my hobbies; why am I interested in them?
- Do these hobbies provide some clues on what I desire in my life?
- Answer a simple question – if I were gifted with all resources and money, what is that one thing I would

like to do? Any constraints that I am putting on myself that are blocking me or not allowing me to think of my Inner Desires.

• Plot your lifeline graph, denote your highs and lows of life and why you felt so? What does your journey say about yourself? When did you overcome challenges and what made you do so? Why was there a push from inside when you took the challenge head-on?

 Remember that to be an extraordinary professional, you need to have a life purpose.

Many a times you find your purpose in a sudden manner. This may be because of a circumstance you're faced with in life; sometimes the purpose is associated with someone else's life too. Or some situation that has occurred in your life could possibly change the direction and give you an indication of your purpose. You would see this many a times in your daily life and around you.

All of our great heroes were never born with a purpose, but circumstances and sufferings made them identify the purpose. Once they identified their purpose, it changed the way they lived, lead, and delivered to the society.

Mahatma Gandhi led the freedom struggle for India; Nelson Mandela led the freedom struggle for South Africa; Abraham Lincoln went through many struggles and eventually became the President of America.

And yes, it is important to keep reviewing your purpose and keep reflecting on the same. Eventually, you will find the true purpose for your own life one day.

Identifying the Purpose:

Sample statements that can guide and help you identify your life purpose:

A life purpose statement describes in clear and full detail the reason why you exist, the impact you are planning to make, and what you would like to be remembered for.

Having a clear idea of your life purpose keeps you motivated, focused, and enables you to tap into a pool of abundant energy your life has to offer.

When you face challenges, you will understand the reasons behind the events in your life, and you start accepting what life has to offer. There cannot be anything more satisfying than this. When you have a purpose, there is no concept of work-life balance, and there is no stress, there is nothing called hard work, there is no more of sitting idle no waiting for any directions. The purpose will start driving the actions in your life.

Some of the possible statements for defining one's life purpose are:

- Being the topmost rated professional in your industry.
- Establishing the business or enabling growth of your business X fold.
- Multiplying your business.
- Aligning with the company purpose and goals and achieving the said goals of the company.
- Providing elderly care to the needy and saving 100,000 lives.
- Providing education to 1 million children.
- Reaching out to the poor and helping them.

- Impacting 10,000 lives and bringing them into the mainstream.
- Put an end to child trafficking.
- Resolving wildlife issues and protecting the animal-life.
- Providing the best transport, if you are in the people transportation business.
- Exploring the world and learning about 100 new cultures and living habits.

 BIGGER THE PURPOSE. HIGHER THE IMPACT, AND LARGER IS YOUR INTERNAL PUSH TO ACHIEVE

Understanding Yourself: The Johari Window

Another tool that is very useful to understand yourself from yours and other people's perspective is the Johari Window. This tool will be useful in getting to know your traits and how others perceive you. This is a very useful tool to introspect and also can lead you to find your own life purpose.

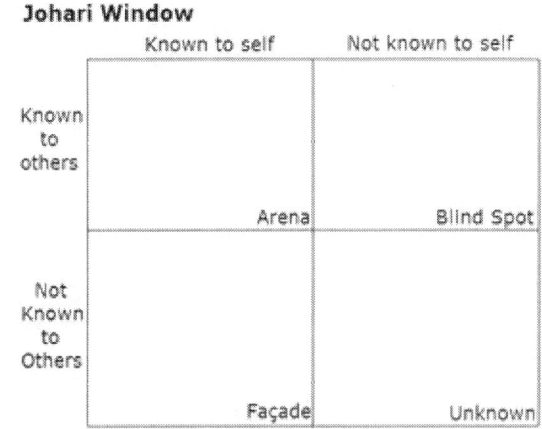

Figure 1 : Johari Window

The Johari window is a technique that helps people understand their relationship with themselves and others better. It was created by psychologists Joseph Luft (1916–2014) and Harrington Ingham (1916–1995) in 1955. Luft and Ingham called their Johari Window model 'Johari' after combining their first names, Joe and Harrington.

To use this tool, gather a set of close friends that know you well and also care about you.

A Johari window uses the following 56 adjectives as possible descriptions of yourself as in the table below.

To do this exercise, first pick a number of adjectives from the above list, choosing ones you feel describe your own personality. Then, request your peers or friends to pick an equal number of adjectives that they think describe you. These adjectives are then inserted into a two-by-two grid of four cells as shown in the figure above.

Able	Clever	Friendly	Introverted
Accepting	Complex	Giving	Kind
Adaptable	Confident	Happy	Knowledgeable
Bold	Dependable	Helpful	Logical
Brave	Dignified	Idealistic	Loving
Calm	Empathetic	Independent	Mature
Caring	Energetic	Ingenious	Modest
Cheerful	Extroverted	Intelligent	Nervous
Observant	Organized	Patient	Powerful
Proud	Quiet	Reflective	Relaxed
Religious	Responsive	Searching	Self-Assertive
Shy	Sensible	Sentimental	Self-Conscious
Silly	Spontaneous	Sympathetic	Tense
Trustworthy	Warm	Wise	Witty

Table 1: Adjective Descriptions

The philosopher Charles Handy calls this concept the Johari House with four rooms.

• Room 1 - Known-Known or also known as the Open/Arena. It is the part of yourself that you and others see. These are your traits that are recognized by all.

• Room 2 – Unknown-Known or also known as Blind Spot contains aspects that others see, but you are unaware of. These are essential traits that are not known to you, but others perceive you as having them. These can often be strengths which can be further nurtured, and may even lead to identifying your purpose.

• Room 3 – Known-Unknown or also known as façade. It is the private space you know but hidden from others. These adjectives are either your own claim of yourself, or you have hidden or not shown to others. You may have to introspect and see why these qualities are not seen by others. They may also provide you with enough insights to see how to nurture them.

• Room 4 - Also known as 'Unknown' is the unconscious part of you that neither ourselves nor others see. The reason could be they do not apply at all or that there is a collective ignorance from all. You can review these adjectives and see if you want to take them up and develop upon.

This exercise may help you in getting to know your traits and what others perceive of you. The focus can be on Room 3, where you feel there are certain traits in you which others don't perceive or see; you may want to strengthen these and create an action plan so that you can openly share these traits with others, helping you build a strong relationship in the process. The Johari window is a great tool to analyze your traits that would also lead to identifying your identity, characteristics, and possibly lead to your purpose.

Once you know your purpose for living, it removes any guesswork and helps you in your decision-making process. The combination of your purpose, your skills, and your life path would guide you to what you truly want from this life.

Once your purpose is identified, explore and start identifying things that will help you build your purpose. For example – the company you will keep, the things you will do, the places you will visit, activities you would do, experiences you will carry, talents you need to build, the knowledge you need to acquire to master the skills.

You may not find the purpose in your first instant, sometimes it takes months or years to truly get your life purpose, and that is fine. But start with a path or combination of some goals that help you set the direction. Once you are on the path to your identified purpose, many things will unfold, and it will finally lead you to identify your true life purpose.

Another important aspect is there could be multiple purposes, one related to your life, one related to your family, one related to society, or one related to your company. Therefore, it is fine to have multiple purposes, just that for every purpose you will need to define a set of goals that align with your purpose.

Once you have used the above tools, questions, introspection techniques, and analysis, you would start identifying your life purpose. Everyone is born unique, and you are no different. This uniqueness and knowledge and your own self will take you to your purpose.

Use the below template to start noting down your learnings from this section and start putting together your LIFE Purpose. Note that this would change, as you continue to read this book and you will find other tools and methods.

By the end of the book, you will be able to refine this purpose and start with some definitive purpose and goals. You will be able to use the foundation values to successfully achieve the same and help you in making your life meaningful.

EXERCISE 1: IDENTIFY PURPOSE

Write your own purpose statement(s)

My Life Purpose Is To:

_____

_____

_____

_____

_____

_____

_____

_____

_____

_____

2

DEFINING THE VISION - WHAT AND WHEN?

IF You can DREAM IT, you can DO IT
— WALT DISNEY

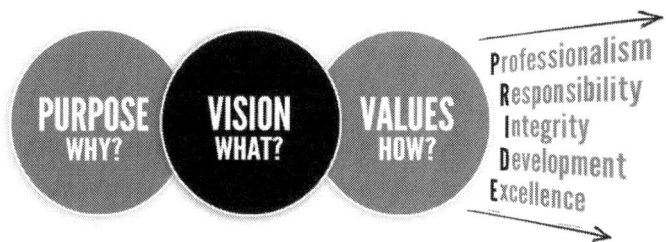

Once you have identified the purpose of your life, it's important to understand the vision and goals you want to achieve, essentially the what and by when?

- What goals are you aiming at?
- Imagine your goals, and understand how your life would be once you reach that goal?
- What path do you need to take to reach your goals?
- What process would you follow to achieve your goals?

If you don't have a goal, these are some questions you can answer to help you define your goal:

- Examine your strengths
- Examine the resources you have (financial, network, people, knowledge)
- Review your purpose and determine what goals you would like to set in order to achieve your defined purpose.

Just like you are going from one train station to another, the goal is to reach the final station you want to go to. Once you know your destination, it's easy to choose the mode and the path you would take. Without knowing the destination, it's difficult to know the path. On same lines, when you are living your life without a purpose and your defined goals, life seems confused, or mundane for many people who are just doing their daily routine without focusing on the goal or destination they want to go to.

As in the above example, just as it is important for you to know the destination, similarly, in life, it's important to have a defined vision/goal.

Using The "SMART" Framework

The November 1981 issue of Management Review contained a paper by George T. Doran called "There's an S.M.A.R.T. way to write goals and objectives." It discussed the importance of objectives and the difficulty of setting them.

The mnemonic S.M.A.R.T. is associated with the process of setting goals. Though there are different adjectives that get referred to sometimes, the most commonly used "SMART" objectives are:

- **Specific** – Goals should be simplistically written and should clearly define what you are going to do.

For Example – GOAL: **To** achieve a career goal of reaching a lead level **by** focusing on the expectations the company has and gaining the necessary skills needed, **so that** it sets a foundation for me to become a manager in next 5 years.

GOAL: **To** help 1 million youths find the jobs they need **by** putting in the framework and tools to gather information of existing jobs, skills, expectations, **so that** we can achieve our set goal by 2020.

- **Measurable** – Goals should be measurable so that you have tangible evidence that you have achieved the goal. There could be multiple elements in the goal statement that you could put, which give you the measurement criteria needed to track your own progress and achieve the same on a timely basis.

GOAL: **To** achieve a career goal of reaching a lead level **by** focusing on the expectations the company has and gaining the necessary skills needed, **so that** it sets a foundation for me to become a manager in next 5 years.

In the above example, the next a 5 years is key aspect and also the element of 'gaining necessary skills' is essential for the measurement criteria.

- **Achievable** – Goals should be achievable. They should be stretched goals at the same time achievable, as stretched goals will challenge and bring the best of you. You must possess or gain the necessary skills, knowledge and abilities needed to achieve the goal.

GOAL: **To** achieve a career goal of reaching a lead level **by** focusing on the expectations the company ha, and gaining the necessary skills needed, **so that** it sets a foundation for me to become a manager in next 5 years.

In the above example, in order to achieve your goal of becoming a manager in the next 5 years, you must possess or acquire the skillset required for this. It could be getting training, or hands-on experience and mastering the skills at a level which can help you take on the manager position. As the skills to be acquired are new, there would be a lot of challenge to acquire them, and as it matches with your goals, you will give your best to achieve those.

- **Relevant** – The goals need to be relevant, ideally in the framework. This relevance should be aligned to your identified purpose.

GOAL: **To** help 1 million youths find the jobs they need **by** putting in the framework and tools to gather information about existing jobs, skills, expectations, **so that** we can achieve our set goal by 2020.

In the above example, if your Life Purpose is impacting a million people, the goal is relevant and aligns to your larger purpose. The more alignments your goals have, the larger the possibility of successfully achieving it.

Time-bound – Specify when the result(s) can be achieved.

GOAL: **To** help 1 million youths find the jobs they need **by** putting in the framework and tools to gather information about existing jobs, skills, expectations, **so that** we can achieve our set goal by 2020.

In above example, by noting down the important dates of 2020, you are forcing yourself to a time-bound action plan that would finally help you achieve your goal. Note that this goal can be further broken down into shorter goals of monthly and quarterly goals that will help you collect all the details, research, and acquire the skills that align with your goals.

The concept of writing S.M.A.R.T. goals is very important for accomplishing individual goals, which in turn are linked to your career, family or financial goals you want to achieve.

 Defining Smart Goals is important to manage your own progress and performance.

THE S-Curve

Sometimes it's difficult to know if your goal is enough to last a long duration. This is the phenomenon with an S-effect. Sometimes what we pursue as a long goal, gets achieved in a shorter time than imagined. Once such goal is done, it's very difficult to maintain that rigor in your life. It's like reaching the peak of the mountain and then thinking about where to go from there? So, in life, it's important that once you get to the top of the S-curve, before the motivation starts tapping down, ensure your new S-curve starts, meaning just before reaching the peak, start the next goal of your life, so that the peak conflict does not occur.

Breaking down into shorter goals.

If you do have a long-term goal of impacting 1 million lives or being a CXO of a company or providing education to 100,000 poor students, it's important that we keep the shorter goals in perspective. More concise goals help in keeping you motivated. The success of achieving a shorter goal is another pull or motivation towards your larger goal. Keep the time scale in mind and focus on shorter goals that need to be met and accomplished.

If you are not able to reach a shorter goal set, or if it is difficult, review again. Maybe divide it again into yet shorter milestones.

 It's not just about setting the goals, you need to set the goals that aligns with your larger purpose, and your passion. By this, I mean enjoy the journey and start celebrating little success that you achieve, so you are motivated enough to go through this long journey.

Pen it Down:

Sometimes it's difficult to have a clear vision and many times opportunities come in different ways to you. Whether you are just walking, watching a movie or just relaxing, an idea strikes you. It's important that you pen this down.

If you already have a goal, then you are set. Ensure you review that periodically and that it is aligned with your purpose. It's important to have a larger goal, and it's equally important to set shorter goals to taste success and help reach the larger goals.

Defining your vision:

Write your vision statement based on the purpose that would guide you, your accomplishments, your legacy, and your glory.

For better preparation of vision, focus on following points:

- What would you like to see yourself as, in 5-10 years?
- What habits would you develop to be the perfect person, living by your vision?
- What are your personal beliefs and values?
- While looking at the vision, take into consideration all the dimensions of your life, like personal, spiritual, emotional, family, social, career and financial. Your vision should align with different dimensions that life offers during the process.
- Just like purpose, you can also have more than one vision elements catering to different aspects, personal, professional, spiritual, family, social, career and financial.

The vision may have one or more points covering the different dimensions, viz,

- A statement to define your career goals
- A statement to define your personal and financial goals
- A statement to define your family goals
- A statement to define your social goals

And many more.

Discovering and implementing your vision is a process of learning, growing in the relationship around you, and fine-tuning. Therefore, your vision is not static. As you start your journey, many things will unfold. The path will start taking shape until you find a true purpose, which would determine and possibly help you refine your vision.

Many people do this exercise at their mid-age, while some start very early on. Note that the earlier you start, the more time you have and therefore, more the chances of achieving your stated vision and purpose. Whenever you start, it's not too late.

 The law of attraction guides you on your path to accomplish what you want.

The following questionnaire will assist you in creating S.M.A.R.T. goals. Begin by writing your goal as clearly and concisely as possible. Then answer the related questions. Conclude by revising your goal in the space allotted. If you have more than one GOAL (ideally should be) use the similar framework and work on the GOALS you would like to have.

While defining the goals, focus on the relevance, as that will help you align with your larger purpose in life. Also every GOAL, will eventually lead to multiples of short-term goals or measurement criteria that would help you achieve a larger GOAL, and hence your purpose.

EXERCISE 2: DEFINE YOUR VISION/GOALS

DEFINE YOUR GOAL:

_____

_____

_____

_____

SPECIFIC: What will the goal accomplish? How and why it will accomplish?

_____

_____

_____

_____

MEASURABLE: List indicators that will help you to measure you're your goals has been reached?

_____

_____

_____

ACHIEVABLE: Are the goals achievable? Do you possess necessary skills, resources, tools, abilities to achieve the goals? What are the gaps and how will you fill that when and how? (Note that this questions will help you define more short-term goals within the large goals)

_____

_____

_____

_____

RELEVANCE: Why are you having this goal? How its relevant to achieve your Life Purpose?

_____

_____

_____

_____

TIME-BOUND: What is the expected dates to complete your goals and do you feel challenged enough that these are stretched goals and will push you to go beyond your normal self to achieve this?

_____

_____

_____

_____

YOUR REVISED VISION/GOAL

_____

_____

_____

_____

_____

_____

_____

_____

_____

_____

_____

_____

_____

_____

_____

_____

_____

_____

_____

_____

_____

_____

_____

_____

_____

PART TWO: VALUES – THE HOW?

Once you have identified the purpose of life and can articulate your long-term vision and goals, it's important to set the values which would guide your behavior.

There are various value systems that we are exposed to:
- Country values,
- Religious value,
- Community values,
- Organization values,
- Family values and
- any other association values we would be connected to.

While all these values are essential to living in this social world, it's essential to define the values that would guide you to be happy and successful in your life. Personal values are those that govern your behavior. Based on my learnings, I have come up with a simple and easy to remember acronym called PRIDE. This acronym would guide you towards creating your own value system which would act as a foundation for your life.

PRIDE in literal meaning means "a feeling of deep pleasure or satisfaction derived from one's achievements, the achievements of one's close associates, or from qualities or possessions that are widely admired."

Hence the PRIDE acronym which would guide your value system will also give you the sense of PRIDE to live this life with dignity, success, and happiness.

The greatest success will happen once your values get aligned with the family values, organization values or the society's values. It is important that you put conscious effort to align these values with people around you and make the best of the same.

The myth about a dream job

Many young professionals look at the company and admire it. They relate well to some of the good qualities of the company environment or a job role. But remember that in this fast-changing world, your dream job may not exist in the next 10-20 years, so it's important you focus on a more significant purpose and goals and then align your business or job to achieve it.

 Try to be unique in whatever way you can. Being unique allows you to be a leader/mentor in your space, rather than being a follower.

An introduction to P.R.I.D.E:

P - Professionalism

The Merriam-Webster dictionary defines professionalism as "the conduct, aims, or qualities that characterize or mark a profession or a professional person";

"Professionalism has to do with the way a person conducts himself or herself in their personal life or at the workplace. An individual who shows consideration and respect for others demonstrates a commitment to professionalism."

> ***Treat people with respect, keep your word, be loyal, and exceed your own and other's expectations.***

R – Responsibility

Responsibility refers to the state or fact of being responsible, answerable, or accountable for something within one's power, control, or management.

Essentially responsibility refers to 3 basic Actions, viz,
- Accept Responsibility for your actions
- Be Accountable for your results
- Take Ownership of your mistakes.

I - Integrity

Integrity refers to the quality of being honest and having strong moral principles.

> ***Integrity helps in building trust and relationships.***

D – Development

Development refers to the wholesome growth of every aspect of your body, mind, and soul.

> ***Development of 'good health', 'powerful mind', and 'blissful soul' is the key to your all-round development.***

E – Excellence

Personal excellence is represented as the ability to create solutions in difficult situations to enable yourself to overcome them. In short, self-management refers to "managing" your own mental and emotional state.

> ***Excel against yourself, not by comparing others.***

In coming chapters, we will focus more on each topic in detail and provide you with actionable steps. You can adapt to and incorporate these values in your life in order to achieve your purpose, vision and thereby lead to a very successful and happy life.

3

PROFESSIONALISM

*CHANGE "I CAN'T" Into "I CAN" and pretty soon you
will say "I DID"*

– Unknown Author

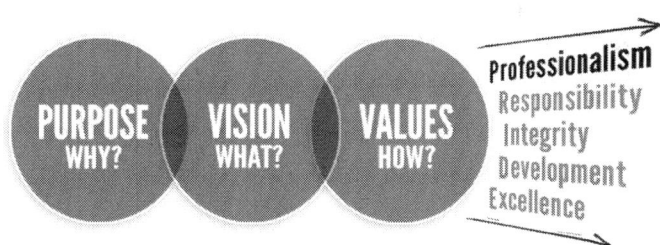

Displaying professionalism is very powerful, it means doing what you have decided. That means living in spirit and not just words. Your actions here do the talk, not your words.

Professionalism shows how serious you are. The stronger commitment you have towards achieving your purpose and vision, the stronger magnet you will become in aligning people with your vision.

Leadership is all about the power to demonstrate your purpose and get an alignment from others to your purpose, making it their purpose as well in a way.

The keys aspects of Professionalism are:

- Treat people with respect
- Keep your word
- Be loyal and
- Exceed your expectations

 The more you "walk the talk," the higher the level of professionalism you achieve; the higher chance you will have towards your success. This requires true discipline. It's hard but not impossible. True heroes who have left a mark in this world lived with the highest level of professionalism.

Think Positive: Think Future: Live in Present

While displaying and actionizing professionalism, it's very important to have a positive state of mind. You should always keep an eye on the future, but you should focus on the present and live for now.

As the saying goes, Your PAST-PERFECT, but your PRESENT-TENSE so enjoy your present.

Smile and be humble

The greatest quality of being professional is to smile and be humble. When you hear about Honourable Abdul Kalam (ex-President of India) the first thing comes to mind is his humbleness. It is said that,

> *"Capability can take you to the top, but humbleness is something which keeps you on top for long."*

A smile is a beautiful gift we all have been given. Even in a tough situation if you smile, it sends a very positive aura in the environment around you. Make the best use of your smile, it relaxes your body, keeping you at ease.

The BIG Picture

A building was getting built, and there were labourers building it. One educated man came near the site and asked one labourer what he was doing, and he said: "I am laying bricks" he moved on and asked another labourer who was also laying the bricks and asked him the same question. This time the second labourer responded by saying "I am building a temple."

This small story provides a simple yet powerful dimension of how we need to look at the big picture. When you are entering a professional world or starting a business of your own, it is important for you to start seeing the big picture. In the context of a project, it's not about writing code, or delivering a letter or completing an accounting sheet. It's mainly about asking yourself:

- Why am I doing what I am doing?

- How does my work impact the larger project, the company?
- Who will all be impacted?
- Do I know the end customers and their expectations?

The more the why's you have, the more you start understanding the big picture.

I am laying bricks – why?
I am constructing a floor – why?

The floor is part of the building, so I am constructing the building. Why?

This building will be used for prayers for the community. Hence I am building a temple.

This is the power of Big Picture.

Be Focussed: Story of the Pregnant Doe

Once, a pregnant doe was walking towards a river, and suddenly she had a deep pain. There was a sudden change in weather, the clouds thundered, and the river started roaring. Suddenly, she saw a big hunter in front of her and heard a roaring lion behind her. Then there was lightning, and the forest near the stream caught fire. She had lost almost all hope. Does she run? If yes, which way? She could not decide. She took a deep breath and decided to focus on delivering the baby. For an instant, she distracted herself from all her surroundings. The hunter began to aim his arrow at the doe. Suddenly, another stroke of lighting came in, and the hunter missed his target. The arrow struck the lion, and the lion died immediately. It started raining heavily, and the forest fire got extinguished. The hunter ran away to find shelter. The Doe delivered the baby and felt happy and relaxed.

So, as you see the same nature that brought all the troubles, brought all the solutions as well. When the doe focussed on her job without getting distracted by external forces, nature supported her and removed the distractions.

In the same way, there will many challenges that will come in your life. But when you are focused, and you are not distracted away from your goals, it helps in staying focused. This would help you build strong professionalism.

Handling Perceptions:

Perception is the identification and interpretation of sensory information in order to represent and understand the presented information or the environment.

How does Perception affect us?

Perception is our sensory experience of the people or environment around us. This involves recognizing environmental stimuli and the actions that are responses to those stimuli. Perception is key to gaining information and understanding the world around us. Without it, we would not be able to survive in this world. Perception not only moulds our experience of the world but also allows us to act within the environment.

During the perception stage, we actually perceive and consciously become aware of the stimulus object that affects us.

It is thought that people differ in the ways that they process information, with each of us having our own unique ways of responding to stimuli. All individuals will react to variable situations in their own specific way.

Perceptions impact the way we judge people, relate to them and start building a mental map of their characteristics and behaviour, which may or may not be real. Once you build certain perceptions of the individual, you start ignoring the context and other's point of view and start focusing on what you see, hear and believe.

The first picture denotes the view from which you are looking at things. There is no right or wrong; it's a viewpoint, based on your context, your success, your experience, and your logic. Note that the other person is also right, as he sees from his side. So, the best way to handle perception is to imagine yourself in the other person's shoes and determine what they are seeing, what they are experiencing and what their logic is. This way you can relate to their context and not hold wrong perceptions. Perceptions are key to increase your level of professionalism. You will not always behave on the basis of your own gut or experience but relate to the context and surroundings. This will help to get as much data as possible for you to make the right decisions.

Look at the picture below. What do you see?

Depending on the angle and focus, it can be seen as an old woman or a young lady, or the image is just an illusion. Development of perception really involves perceiving new objects in the old (bringing in a new dimension or a radical thought).

A moment's reflection will show the similarity of this fact to analysing attention, i. e., to continue giving our attention to an object for more than a moment, we notice something new about it, see it in a new way. We might, of course, substitute the word perception for the word 'attention', and then the proposition would read: we cannot continue to perceive an object beyond a moment or two, unless we perceive it in a new manner.

Perceptions which we do not execute in a new way tend to lapse from our consciousness, passing over into habits of response which we make to certain physical stimuli.

When you come across a challenge and feel stuck in one place, you need to change your own perspective and start seeing things from a different perspective (maybe from other individual points of view). This will help you look at the challenge in a new manner, analyse and enable you to create a better solution.

Handling perceptions also help you become very strong professionally as it reduces your bias. It allows you to think objectively, empowers you to collect all the information from yourself, others and surroundings, which enables a better decision-making process.

Non-Judgemental Awareness

Non-Judgemental Awareness is a tool which helps you to look at things from other's perspective and help in managing perception better. An old saying that goes "Put yourself in other's shoes" seems apt here.

This important and simple attribute helps you determine things as they are, understand other's perspective, transform the dimension, and help you be more collaborative.

Remember that your judgments would be based on:

- Perceived notions
- Perceptions about a person
- Past experience and learnings of your own
- Your track records
- Your interactions and deriving insights from that data
- Your beliefs and habits.

So when you are in situations where you feel lost or you think no one is listening to you, it is essential to use the Non-Judgemental Awareness and focus your view on looking at the other side. This will help you become humbler and display a high level of professionalism.

STORY: The 5 BLIND MEN and the ELEPHANT

Once upon a time, five blind men came across an elephant.

"What is this?" asked the first one, who had run headfirst into its side.

"It's an elephant." said the elephant's keeper, who was sitting on a stool, cleaning the elephant's harness.

"Wow, so this is an elephant! I've always wondered what elephants are like." said the man, running his hands as far as he could reach, up and down the elephant's side. "Why, it's just like a wall, a large, warm wall!"

"What do you mean, a wall?" said the second man, wrapping his arms around the elephant's leg. "This is nothing like a wall. You can't reach around a wall! This is more like a pillar. Yeah, that's it, an elephant is exactly like a pillar!"

"A pillar? Strange kind of pillar!" said the third man, stroking the elephant's trunk. "It's too thin, for one thing, and it's too flexible for another. If you think this is a pillar, I don't want to go to your house! This is more like a snake. See, it's wrapping around my arm. An elephant is just like a snake!"

"Snakes don't have hair!" said the fourth man in disgust, pulling the elephant's tail. "You are closer than the others, but I'm surprised that you missed the hair. This isn't a snake, it's a rope. Elephants are exactly like ropes."

"I don't know what you guys are on!" the fifth man cried, waving the elephant's ear back and forth. "It's as large as a wall, all right, but thin as a leaf, and no more flexible than any piece of cloth this size should be. I don't know what's wrong with all of you, but no one except a complete idiot could mistake an elephant for anything except a sail!"

And as the elephant moved on, they stumbled along down the road, arguing more vehemently as they went, each sure that he, and he alone, was right and all the others were wrong. Whereas the truth is that an elephant is… an elephant.

How many times do we argue about the details of things but looking at the bigger picture would have saved a lot of debate?

Great leaders are able to bring people with diverse perspectives and personalities together to help them understand that although they may only experience a certain part of the elephant, it's still an elephant.

> The next time you debate with someone at your work, check yourself to make sure that you're not at the trunk end when your peer is holding the tail.

Effective Listening

The most significant communication problem is we do not listen to understand, but we listen to reply.

Active listening means focussing on the content and not the person. When you have a bias against someone or if you hate someone, you always have a preconceived notion of what you believe is being said, then what is actually said. This is called selective listening. It distracts you from understanding the real content that is actually being said. This is true when you are receiving feedback; your focus tends to be the person who is providing the feedback and not the feedback itself.

To increase your power of listening with a focus on Non-Judgemental Awareness, try this simple technique:

> Focus on the sounds around you. Don't try to describe the object or nature that is creating the sound, instead just focus on the sound. Don't think of water flowing or a bird chirping, or an animal making a sound but focus on just the sound and let the sound fill you with joy and content. This simple technique, when practiced regularly, will help you focus, improve your effective listening, and help you to practice Non-Judgemental Awareness.

This technique will also help you deal with people effectively, remove any biases and also remove the urge of responding without listening and understanding.

> *When you talk, you repeat what you already know. But when you listen, you will learn a new thing you might not know.*

Solve this question:

"You are driving a bus. At the first stop, 8 people get on the bus. At the next stop 10 people get off the bus and 6 people get on." What is the age of the driver?

The answer is in the question itself, if you have not understood the question, read again. Effective listening is an art. Listen to things that are being talked about, this will help you gather more data and may help you make an informed decision.

Take risks but learn from your mistakes:

"Take risks in your life, if you WIN, you can LEAD! If you Lose, you can GUIDE!" – Swami Vivekananda

> *Good judgment comes with experience but experience comes from mistakes.*

Risks are good. You should take risks, as they pull you out of your comfort zone and allow you to scale and achieve greater heights. Remember that it is okay to make mistakes. Some people may get furious, like your boss, but realize that this will help you build experience and also help in dealing with ambiguities in your personal and professional life.

The Story of Two Seeds:

Two seeds lay side by side in the fertile spring soil.

The first said, "I want to grow! I want to send my roots deep into the soil beneath me, and thrust my sprouts through the earth's crust above me. I want to unfurl my tender buds like banners to announce the arrival of spring. I want to feel the warmth of the sun on my face and the bliss of the morning dew on my petals!"

And she grew.

The second seed said, "I am afraid. If I send my roots into the ground below, I don't know what I will encounter in the dark. If I push my way through the hard soil above me I may damage my delicate sprouts. What if I let my buds open and a snail tries to eat them? And if I were to open my blossoms, a small child may pull me from the ground. No, it is much better for me to wait until it is safe."

And so she waited.

A yard hen scratching around in the early spring ground for food found the waiting seed and promptly ate it.

Those of us who refuse to risk and grow get swallowed by life.

Hope you've got an understanding of Professionalism now and understood how you could use your learnings to become more professional.

Note down your learning in the below template. Identify your current state and your desired state, so that you can

come up with an action plan to build a foundation of
Professionalism in your life.

EXERCISE 3: PROFESSIONALISM

List down your current state of professionalism, desired state and the actions you will take to move from current state to desired state

CURRENT STATE

_____

_____

_____

_____

DESIRED STATE

_____

_____

_____

_____

ACTIONS

_____

_____

_____

4

RESPONSIBILITY

*Responsibility Equals Accountability Equals Ownership.
Sense of Ownership is the most powerful weapon a
team or organization can have.*

— *Pat Summit.*

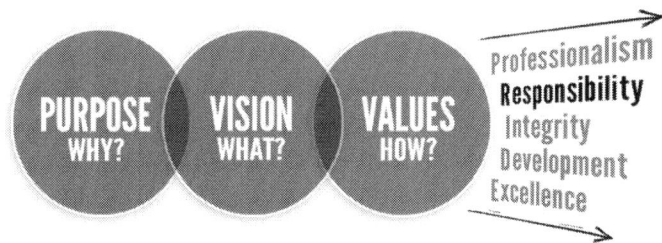

Commitment: The Doctor Story

A young child met with an accident. He was taken to the

hospital. His father was called from work, and he came rushing to the hospital. They were seated for two hours, and the father got extremely angry. Then he suddenly saw the doctor rushing in. Reacting in anger, the man started scolding the doctor and used many harsh words for him and his family. The doctor quietly went inside, changed his clothes, and went and operated on the child. After almost 3 hours, the surgery was successful, and the child was saved. The doctor came out and informed the man. The man was still angry though happy with the result, and he asked the doctor in a harshly,

"What if my child would have died? You came in 2 hours late!."

The doctor replied, "My father had an attack in the morning, and he passed away. I came here immediately after attending his funeral as I was informed of this case and there were no other doctors around. So as a professional, it was my responsibility to come here and operate on the child."

There was a deep silence.

There are certain definite measures you can take to increase your own responsibility and shape your own behavior so that you build a responsible foundation for your life:

- Show commitment in actions, not just in words
- Take ownership of your actions
- Take responsibility for your mistakes, learn from mistakes and don't repeat them.
- Commitment to family and friends
- Review and keep your calendar for the day
- Set a clear agenda and outcome for your meetings
- Take responsibility for your words, your work and your life.

Enjoy what you do/your work:

It's important that you enjoy your work and don't treat it like any other mundane task.

• Find people that align with your goals, or you can align your goal to someone's vision. When things are aligned, you enjoy the workplace, people around you, and the work.

• Find problems you enjoy solving. You have certain strengths. You may be a good negotiator, a good marketing person , a good sales hunter. Finding a problem that you can solve will increase the level of your passion and help you become more responsible.

Time Management: Using Time Effectively and Not Just Efficiently

In a 1954 speech to the Second Assembly of the World Council of Churches, former U.S. President Dwight D. Eisenhower, who was quoting Dr. J. Roscoe Miller, president of Northwestern University, said: "I have two kinds of problems: the urgent and the important. The urgent is not important, and the important is never urgent." This "Eisenhower Principle" explains how he organized his workload and priorities.

He recognized that great time management means being effective as well as efficient. In other words, we must spend our time on things that are important and not just the ones that are urgent. To do this and to minimize the stress of having too many tight deadlines, we need to understand this distinction:

• Important activities have an outcome that leads us towards achieving our goals, whether these are professional or personal.

- Urgent activities demand immediate attention and are usually associated with achieving someone else's goals. They are often the ones that demand attention and the ones we concentrate on because the consequences of not dealing with them are immediate.

When we know, the distinction between the activities are important and those that are urgent, we can overcome the natural tendency to focus on unimportant urgent activities. This will help us clear enough time to do what is essential for our success. This is the way we move from "firefighting" mode into a position, where we can focus and achieve our desired goals.

Using Eisenhower's Principle:

To use this principle, list all of the activities and projects that you feel you have to do. Try to include everything that takes up your time at work, however unimportant.

Next, think about each activity and put it into one of four categories.

FIGURE 4 : Time Management Matrix

Then use the strategies described below to schedule your activities.

1. Important and Urgent

There are two distinct types of urgent and important activities: ones that you could not have foreseen, and others that you've left until the last minute.

You can eliminate last minute activities by planning ahead and avoiding procrastination.

However, you can't always predict or avoid some issues and crises. Here, the best approach is to leave some time in your schedule to handle unexpected issues and important unplanned activities. (If a major crisis arises, then you'll need to reschedule other tasks.)

If you have a lot of urgent and important activities,

identify which of these you could have foreseen, and think about how you could schedule similar activities ahead of time, so that they don't become urgent.

2. Important but Not Urgent

These are the activities that help you achieve your personal and professional goals and complete important work.

Make sure that you have plenty of time to do these things properly so that they do not become urgent. Also, remember to leave enough time in your schedule to deal with unforeseen problems. This will maximize your chances of keeping on track, and help you avoid the stress of work becoming more urgent than necessary.

3. Not Important but Urgent

Urgent but not important tasks are things that prevent you from achieving your goals. Ask yourself whether you can reschedule or delegate them.

A common source of such activities is other people. Sometimes it's appropriate to say "No" to people politely or to encourage them to solve the problem themselves.

Alternatively, try to have time slots when you are available so that people know they can speak with you then. A good way to do this is to arrange regular meetings with those who interrupt you often so that you can deal with all their issues at once. You'll then be able to concentrate on your important activities for longer.

4. Not Important and Not Urgent

These activities are just a distraction – avoid them if possible.

You can simply ignore or cancel many of them. However, some may be activities that other people want you to do, even though they don't contribute to your own desired outcomes. Again, say "no" politely, if you can, and explain why you cannot do it.

If people see that you are clear about your objectives and boundaries, they will often avoid asking you to do "not important" activities in the future.

Maintain a good to-do list:

There are many ways you can manage your to-do lists. I keep following these two to manage my tasks:

Pen-it-down: I keep a post-it at my home and office to list down any tasks that I remember, or need to act on, based on mail response, or actions that I need to complete. If you are very hands-on with your mobile, there are various apps now that will help you keep track of your tasks.

Calendar: Calendars are the best way to manage our scheduled and repeated tasks and also manage tasks that need to be done on a particular date. Reviewing your calendar at the start of the week always helps in keeping your week focussed. Ensure that there are tasks related to your Long Term and Short Term Goals in your calendar. Make sure you bring in the sense of seriousness to complete this tasks along with all other priorities that come from your environment. That is the only way you can be responsible, accountable and also keep your focus on achieving your larger purpose.

Every task in the to-do lists has attributes like - importance, priority, completion timeline, and the value of the tasks. It is important to look at all these attributes.

Once you have analysed your tasks in different buckets, some will find their way into your calendar, and some will just get dropped.

I plan my calendar by looking at the forthcoming week on a Sunday evening. I analyse the progress I have made on my goals. I keep specific actions to be performed on my calendar to ensure that I progress towards my goals. It is also good to analyse your day at the end of each day, do a quick review of your progress versus the plan you had for the day.

Embracing Change

"You must take personal responsibility. You cannot change the circumstances, the seasons or the wind, but you can change yourself" – Jim Rohn.

Remember: Change is the only constant in life. It's important you embrace the change and make it a part of life. The moment you go into a comfort zone, external forces will start taking over, and you will start losing your position.

The most important reasons for embracing change are:

- **Making a change gives me the chance to grow**. I have a hard time realizing personal growth if I continue to do the same things every day.
- **Change makes me stronger**. Not all changes are beneficial, but there are always positives that can be found in them. I become stronger by learning to overcome the challenges that change the present.
- **Change teaches me how to be flexible and more open to compromise**. When I have to look a little harder for solutions, it helps me grow.
- **Some changes are necessary for personal, physical, and mental health**. Realizing I need to

drop a few pounds or that I need to connect with people who support me can help with monitoring bad habits that steal my confidence.

- **The change gives me something new to look forward to**. Change offers new adventures and the opportunity to learn more life lessons.
- **Change is one way to move forward with the goals I've set**. Without change, I feel stuck and uninspired.
- **The change allows me to grow spiritually**. Remembering to lift my head from the busyness and leaning on faith changes my outlook on life for the better.
- **Change helps me build new relationships**. I meet people I wouldn't have been able to meet without seeking change.
- **The change gives me the opportunity to stretch my wings and learn more about the world**. I discover new interests, passions, and talents that make life more complete.

STORY: The Wise Man and the Star Fish

Once upon a time, there was a wise man that used to go to the ocean to do his writing. He had a habit of walking on the beach before he started his work.

One day, as he was walking along the shore, he looked down at the beach and saw a human figure moving like a dancer. As a result, he walked faster to catch up with this individual.

As he got closer, he noticed that the figure was of a young man and he was not dancing after all. He was reaching down to the shore, picking up small objects and throwing them into the ocean.

As he approached, he called out "Good morning. May I ask what it is that you are doing?"

The young man paused, looked up, and replied "Throwing starfish into the ocean."

"I must ask, then, why are you throwing starfish into the ocean?" asked the somewhat startled writer.

To this, the young man replied, "The sun is up, and the tide is going out. If I don't throw them in, they'll die."
Upon hearing this, the writer commented, "But, young man, do you not realize that there are miles and miles of beach, and there are starfish along every mile? You can't possibly make a difference!"

At this, the young man bent down, picked up yet another starfish and threw it into the ocean. As it sank into the ocean, he said: "It made a difference for that one."

Moving out of your comfort zone

It's important that you don't make your daily routine a mundane one. If the same tasks are repeating day after day, you will lose motivation, and that will impact your performance.

Once you feel that you are getting in a comfort zone, do something that is weird and different from your daily routine.

Get engaged in a sport of your choice, do some adventure activities, prepare to run the marathon, learn a new language, join a meditation or spiritual class.

The moment you do something different, it means you are taking risks, and it will allow you to move out from your comfort zone. These activities will then help you focus more on work and remove the mundane syndrome from your work/business/life.

Similarly, if you feel you are not moving towards your larger vision/goal, remember to break your larger goal into shorter goals. As you start achieving your short-term goals, this moves you out from your comfort zone and allows you to pass through your fears or interferences.

In life, there will be instances when you feel completely bored, you feel your life is at a standstill, and you don't enjoy what you're doing. This is the time to introspect, review your goals, and realign your actions to achieve your goal. Remember that stress will take over if you don't control your own life and time.

Receiving timely feedbacks

Feedback from your loved ones is a good way to change yourself and your habits. It's very difficult to see yourself through another person's eyes, so honest feedback would allow that insight and help you improve your habits and be more responsible.

Remember that we are all human and human beings find it tough to give and receive feedback. Many of us get defensive when we hear feedback. Many people also assume that no one would like to hear feedback from them, so they stop themselves from giving that crucial feedback.

> Constructive criticism is an important ingredient for personal and professional development and for strengthening relationships. Whether it's from your boss, a mentor, an executive coach, family or close relatives, or even from anonymous surveys, being receptive to feedback is essential.

Here are some principles that can guide towards getting effective feedback:

Active Listening – Listen to what is being said and ask questions to clarify your doubts. Summarize the feedback so that you really take in what is being said or told.

Never Argue, Just say Thanks: Arguing derails the discussion and will not allow the person to complete the feedback. They will form a perception that you are not so receptive. By doing so, you will miss something important that may have helped you. Even if they are wrong, there is no reason to argue or defend yourself. Just remember that this is the perception the person has carried about you. End the discussion with "Thanks" and reflect on why that person gave you that feedback, introspect, analyse and change your actions/habits/patterns to overcome that.

Evaluate and Analyze the Feedback – Don't just act on the feedback or accept it or reject it, take your time to analyze it, ask for more data, or look at patterns of your behaviour. Are there more than one people that have given you this feedback? Is it your habit or your unconscious behaviour?

Close the LOOP – Be conscious of the feedback. Once you have analysed it and have worked on it, remember to go back to the person who gave you that feedback, and see if you can close the loop with the person. Believe me; this is very satisfying.

Being Accountable

Accountability is the glue that ties commitment to results.

It's not just important to be committed but being accountable also considers the results that come out as a result of your commitment. Your hard work is not enough, but smart work that enables results is what matters the most.

Seldom you will come across situations where you feel you have given your best, but you are not getting that deserved recognition, etc. Accept the fact that if results don't come in, there is a need to introspect, probably change a path or an approach, and accept the failure even after your full commitment.

> *You can't hold people accountable unless you demonstrate accountability yourself.*

Story on Accountability:

This is a story about four people named Everybody, Somebody, Anybody, and Nobody. There was an important job to be done, and Everybody was asked to do it. Everybody was sure Somebody would do it. Anybody could have done it, but Nobody did it. Somebody got angry about this because it was Everybody's job. Everybody thought Anybody could do it, but Nobody realized that Everybody wouldn't do it. It ended up in a situation where Everybody blamed Somebody when Nobody did what Anybody could have done.

A person who is ACCOUNTABLE is the one ultimately answerable for the correct and thorough completion of the task. He is the one who delegates work to those responsible for completing it. In other words, an 'accountable' must sign off (approve) work that 'responsible provides.'

THE RACI MODEL – Responsible, Accountable, Consulted and Informed

Responsibility Assignment Matrix - RACI Chart

	Jeff	Michael	Rollo	YOU	Alex	Anna	Bill	Cindy	Katie	Fred	Hans	John	Livio	Luc	Marco	Paul	Peter	Sue	Ted	Tim
Planning / Schedule	R	A	I	C				C												Q
Risk Management	I	I	Q								A							R		
Quality Management			R	C							R									A
Procurement			R		Q						R							R		A
1. Specifications Listing							A		R									R		R
2. Site Requirements	C	A	R	Q								R								
3. Call for Tenders			Q	A	R	C						R						R		
4. Budget Approval			A	Q							R					R				R
5. Contract Negotiations		A		Q	R	R												R		

* R – Responsible (works on), A – Accountable, C – Consulted, I – Informed, Q – Quality Reviewer

FIGURE 5 : RACI CHART

A responsibility assignment Matrix also is known as a RACI Model describes the actors in various roles in completing tasks or deliverables for a project, assignment, or a goal. It is especially useful in clarifying roles and responsibilities in an organization or your business. It promotes accountability since for any task there would be only one Accountable Person.

In a typical RACI Chart, at least one Responsible person and exactly one Accountable person are designated for each task. There could be Optional Consulted and Informed roles that may be added based on the support needed to complete the tasks.

Key Responsibility Roles:

R=Responsible, A=Accountable, C=Consulted, I=Informed

- *Responsible* (also *Recommender*)

Those who do the work to complete the task. There is at least one role with a participation type of responsible, although others can be delegated to assist in the work required.

- *Accountable* (also *Approver* or *final approving authority*)

The one is ultimately answerable for the correct and thorough completion of the deliverable or task. The one who ensures the prerequisites of the task are met and the one who delegates the work to those responsible. In other words, an accountable must sign off (approve) work that responsibly provides. There must be only one accountable specified for each task or deliverable.

- *Consulted* (sometimes *Consultant* or *counsel*)

Those whose opinions are sought, typically subject matter experts; and with whom there is two-way communication.

- *Informed* (also *Informee*)

Those who are kept up-to-date on progress, often only upon completion of the task or deliverable, and with whom there is just one-way communication.

There is a distinction between a role and individually identified people: a role is a descriptor of an associated set of tasks; may be performed by many people, and one person can perform many roles. For example, an organization may have ten people who can perform the role of project manager, although traditionally each project only has one project manager at any one time, and a person who is able to perform the role of project manager may also be able to perform other roles.

Hope you've now got an understanding of Responsibility and how you can use your learnings to become more Responsible and Accountable. Note down your learning in the below template. Identify your current state and your desired state, so that you can come up with an action plan to build a foundation of Responsibility in your life.

> *The goals and measurement criteria help you keep track of your progress, and hence it's important to have measurable milestones for your journey.*

EXERCISE 4: RESPONSIBILITY

List down your current state of responsibility, desired state and the actions you will take to move from current state to desired state.

CURRENT STATE

_____

_____

_____

_____

DESIRED STATE

_____

_____

_____

_____

ACTIONS

_____

_____

_____

SANDEEP AGARWAL

5

INTEGRITY

Honesty is making your words confirm to Reality;
Integrity is making reality confirm to your words.

– Stephen Covey

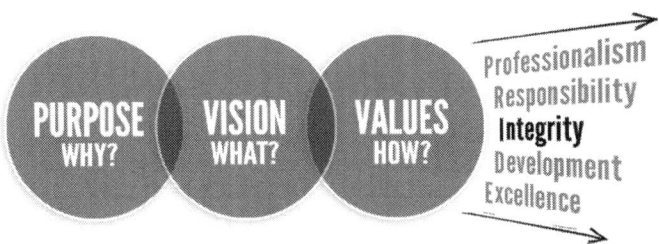

Feed the good self: The good and bad wolf

Every person has two wolves within themselves; there is one good wolf and one a bad wolf. It's always a 50% share that both wolves have within you. There is a good side of you, and there is a bad side of you. So which wolf wins? The one that you feed the most. Feed the good one, and you will be honest, humble, and kind. Feed the bad one, and you will be angry, sad, and frustrated. – Extract from one of Mr. Prem Rawat's excerpts.

Being honest and trustworthy [1]:

A successful businessman was growing old and knew it was time to choose a successor to take over the business.

Instead of choosing one of his directors or his children, he decided to do something different. He called all the young executives in his company together.

He said, "It is time for me to step down and choose the next CEO. I have decided to choose one of you."

The young executives were shocked, but the boss continued. "I am going to give each one of you a seed today – one very special seed, I want you to plant the seed, water it, and come back here one year from today with what you have grown from the seed I have given you. I will then judge the plants that you bring, and the one I choose will be the next CEO."

One man, named Jim, was there that day and he, like the others, received a seed. He went home and excitedly told his wife the story. She helped him get a pot, soil, and compost and he planted the seed. Every day, he would water it and watch to see if it had grown. After about three weeks, some of the other executives began to talk about their seeds and the plants that were beginning to grow.

---

[1]Source: http://www.beautifulquotes.co/2016/09/how-one-ceo-taught-his-employees-lesson.html

Jim kept checking his seed, but nothing ever grew.

Three weeks, four weeks, five weeks went by, still nothing.

By now, others were talking about their plants, but Jim didn't have a plant, and he felt like a failure.

Six months went by — still nothing in Jim's pot. He just knew he had killed his seed. Everyone else had trees and tall plants, but he had nothing. Jim didn't say anything to his colleagues, however.
He just kept watering and fertilizing the soil.

A year went by, and all the young executives of the company brought their plants to the CEO for inspection.

Jim told his wife that he wasn't going to take an empty pot. But she asked him to be honest about what had happened. Jim felt sick to his stomach. It was going to be the most embarrassing moment of his life, but he knew his wife was right. He took his empty pot to the boardroom. When Jim arrived, he was amazed at the variety of plants grown by the other executives. They were beautiful — in all shapes and sizes. Jim put his empty pot on the floor, and many of his colleagues laughed, a few felt sorry for him!

When the CEO arrived, he surveyed the room and greeted his young executives.

Jim just tried to hide in the back. "My, what great plants, trees, and flowers you have grown," said the CEO. "Today one of you will be appointed the next CEO!"

All of a sudden, the CEO spotted Jim at the back of the room with his empty pot. He ordered the Financial Director to bring him to the front. Jim was terrified. He thought, "The CEO knows I'm a failure! Maybe he will have me fired!"

When Jim got to the front, the CEO asked him what had happened to his seed – Jim told him the story.

The CEO asked everyone to sit down except Jim. He looked at Jim, and then announced to the young executives, "Behold your next Chief Executive Officer!

His name is Jim!" Jim couldn't believe it. Jim couldn't even grow his seed.
"How could he be the new CEO?" the others said.

Then the CEO said, "One year ago today, I gave everyone in this room a seed. I told you to take the seed, plant it, water it, and bring it back to me today. But I gave you all boiled seeds; they were dead – it was not possible for them to grow.

All of you, except Jim, have brought me trees and plants and flowers. When you found that the seed would not grow, you substituted another seed for the one I gave you. Jim was the only one with the courage and honesty to bring me a pot with my seed in it. Therefore, he is the one who will be the new Chief Executive Officer!"

- Plant honesty- reap trust
- Plant goodness - reap friends
- Plant humility- reap greatness
- Plant perseverance - reap contentment
- Plant consideration - reap perspective
- Plant hard work - reap success
- Plant forgiveness - reap reconciliation
- Plant faith in God - reap Harvest

So, be careful what you plant now, it will determine what you will reap later.

"Whatever you give to life, life gives back to you."

Avoid Distractions:

At many times you will be distracted by things that can provide you with personal gains, compared to what is right. Allow your good wolf to take charge and avoid these distractions, and you will always feel good and happy. At the same time, you will be building trust and attracting a lot of people that would bring in opportunities for larger things.

Especially when you have a defined purpose in life and have set yourself for an ambitious goal, remember that integrity is the only way that you will enjoy your journey. It will help you avoid stress and march on towards your goal. However strong you are, keep in mind that you cannot achieve things on your own. We are social beings, and we need to have aligned company of like-minded people that can help us achieve our goals or purpose.

Remove noise: Build solid foundations.

There will be many instances you will come across smaller issues or noises. Ensure that you are not distracted by these noises. There might be downs in your life, and bad wolf inside you may start taking over. Keep your focus, feed the good wolf, and you will build a solid foundation. No high rise building can be built without having a solid foundation; no strong tree grows without having strong roots. To understand the principles of nature and create a life with utmost integrity.

Once upon a time, there were two men and each needed to build a house.

The first man was foolish. He chose to build on sandy soil where the soil was easy to access and easy to dig the foundations. In a few short weeks, he was almost finished.

The second man was wise. He chose to build his house on

a rocky hill, where it was very hard to access and to dig the foundation. He spent many months building his house.

As time passed a huge storm broke upon the houses of these men. After much rain, a flood swept through the valley, and the man's house that was built on sand was swept away. But the second man who had built on the rocky hill was safe. No matter how hard it rained or how fierce the floods were his house remained solid and immovable.

Let's ask ourselves the question: What's the foundation of our life? Are we like the foolish man, are we building our lives on sand?

Trust: The Most Valuable Business Commodity: [David Williams, Forbes contributor]

To succeed as a business, you must assess the quality of relationships across your organization—from leaders to employees, employees to leaders, employees to employees, and employees to customers. Do the individuals in all of these groups honour and respect one another, or are they neglected and considered unimportant?

You'll always be able to see, hear, and feel when trusting relationships exist in organizations. A healthy organization is full of people who:

- Are loyal to one another. They keep their word and honor their journey.
- Never judge -- seek first to understand.
- Laugh with (not at) others.
- Take up issues directly with the concerned people and not talk behind others' backs.
- Express genuine appreciation up, down, and across their organizational structure.

- Help others with critical tasks. You don't hear, "That's not my job" in a successful organization. You hear, "We're in this together."
- Recognize that people aren't problems—problems are problems. People who have been hurt sometimes turn around and hurt other people. They need to see beyond the hurt and help others instead.
- Smile frequently. People should leave work happier than when they arrived.
- Don't start sentences or thoughts with, "What's in it for me?" but with, "How can I serve you?"

> ***Strong relationships are based on trust. Organizations can build a culture of trust by cultivating honesty and integrity in workers' interactions.***

Here are five questions to ask that will help you measure the quality of a company's promises:

- How committed are team members in keeping their obligations? The answers to this question are generally evident: When leaders and employees make and keep their promises, they see strong trust and respect across the organization. If they frequently make commitments but fail to keep them, they see frustration and self-serving behaviour.
- Do employees hold peers accountable for their commitments? In an environment of trust, people are free and have the confidence to be direct and assertive when promises are missed, and quick to thank others when they're kept.
- What happens when circumstances are the cause of people failing to keep commitments? Ideally, the promiser should update all stakeholders so that they

know well in advance, and should do all that they can to move to an appropriate and acceptable "Plan B." The promisor could even enlist the stakeholders in helping them arrive at a mutually acceptable "Plan C."

- Do team members consider promises to customers to be no more and no less important than their promises to peers? Think about this closely. If it is easy to forget a promise to a co-worker, it is just as easy to neglect a promise to a customer as well. The continuum runs in both directions, wherever you are.

- Is everyone at your organization willing to forgive themselves and one another? Sometimes it's easier to forgive others than it is to extend that grace to yourself. Similar to the principle of self-respect we need to learn to smile at our shortcomings and forgive our own follies as we work to grow and succeed continually.

In summary, these are the traits, and these are the critical questions to ask; as you examine the culture in your own place of work. If trust is lacking, take the necessary steps to allow this vital aspect to improve. The foundation of trust will permeate every aspect of your company: the people, the products they produce, and the corporate culture. This is why we consider trust to be a non-negotiable trait.

Hope that you have an understanding of Integrity and know how you can use your learnings to live your life with utmost Integrity.

Note down your learning in the below template. Identify your current state and your desired state, so that you can come up with an action plan to build a foundation of Integrity in your life.

EXERCISE 5 : INTEGRITY

List down your current state of integrity, desired state and the actions you will take to move from current state to desired state

CURRENT STATE

_____

_____

_____

_____

DESIRED STATE

_____

_____

_____

_____

ACTIONS

_____

_____

_____

6

DEVELOPMENT

The capacity to learn is a GIFT;
the ability to learn is a SKILL;
the willingness to learn is a CHOICE

— Brian Herbert

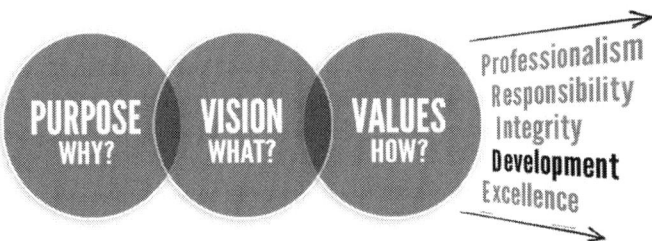

In the Knowledge Era that we are in, the whole emphasis is on building your knowledge and skills to keep you relevant to the changing demands of this market and environment. There is so much demand that people are learning new courses and getting trained to be multi-skilled. People have forgotten their body and soul by only focusing on the mind.

The new age technologies also emphasize on the usage of the mind so much that there are lifestyle and health issue popping up. People have become more distanced from their self.

Body, mind, and soul are inter-related. You have a responsibility to act on all 3 aspects, viz.

- Duty to the body – keeping it healthy and fit
- Duty to the mind – developing its focus and powers
- Duty to the soul – daily meditation to keep it calm and mindful.

Ask Questions

The greatest way you can learn is to be open to ask questions. Many projects fail because people fear to ask questions. They make assumptions and in the end, find that they have missed some crucial information.

The man who asks the question is a fool for a minute, the man who does not ask the question is a fool for a life – Confucius.

One day I was traveling to the US and was quite tired due to a hectic business trip. I was at the check-in counter, and the lady was helping me with my boarding pass. I was not a priority customer, and our company policies did not allow business class travel. I was very hesitant to ask for an upgrade. Finally, I mustered some courage, smiled and asked the lady at the desk if she can help me get a free upgrade. The lady looked at me, was astonished at first, gazed at me, waited for a minute and said: "Let me ask my manager." She went inside, and to my surprise, she came back with a yes! She said that the plane was only half full, so she could honor my request this time. What if I would not have dared to ask the question?

Don't imitate others, be yourself.

It's important to have self-belief. Many people create role models and try to change themselves to model others. While it is important to look at some of the qualities of a role model, it is essential that you keep your own identity in perspective. You are born unique, and you are not the other person. Look at the best habits people have or the actions great people have taken and create your unique list of attributes. At the place of your professional work, people try to imitate another person, thinking if they work like them, they would be rewarded or promoted as well. Note that this is a myth. You need to compete with yourself and not with someone else. You are born unique, and you create your own identity.

 Remember that you have to drive to your purpose. *Ask the question – what should people remember you for after you die?*

20:20:20 Rule

To focus on your complete growth, for your mind, body, and soul, you need to spend time with yourself every single day. I practice a 20:20:20 rule every day.

Many people focus on just body, going to the gym, running, exercises to keep their body fit. Others look at meditation as the sole way to keep them energized and rejuvenated. Some keep on improving their mind power. While there are many schools of thought on what is better and what is not, and many research papers discuss the benefit of one versus another, the critical aspect is that you need a bit of everything.

For me, a 20:20:20 rule means an hour every day with yourself. 20 minutes of exercise to keep your body fit. 20 minutes of reading mind exercises to keep your mind sharp and energized. 20 minutes of meditation, going deep and hearing what your soul has to say to you. This translates into an hour of rejuvenation, complete reset, which enables you to be in the moment called "now." Remember that a healthy body, focused mind, and blissful soul will make you Mindful being,

This 20:20:20 rule is good if your ambition or a professional job does not involve doing one of the above for a living itself. For example, if you are a meditation teacher or a gym trainer, you will, of course, spend much more of your time on those activities.

Disconnect from the digital world:

In this highly connected and digital world, it is important for you to disconnect. The frequency of disconnection and the duration depends on the workload and stress you are going through. A general rule of thumb is that you take a break for at least a half a day every week. Choose the best time/day that suits you and make it a habit not to be connected to your mobile, emails, calls or meetings). The time can be spent with family/friends, or just cooling or relaxing your mind. If you are on a 5-day work routine, then Saturday any half day would work best to be digitally disconnected, as Sunday you can use for review, and get warmed up for your upcoming week plans.

Beyond the weekly routine, I would suggest a vacation with family at least once a year for a week. This is where you explore a new place, learn a new culture, get down to enjoying the nature. Your family and kids need time. They get an exposure to nature; nature is the best healer and the best teacher. Understand what the place has to offer from a traditional point of you and explore the same.

Learn from unusual sources:

If you are an engineer the chances are that you will explore more engineering elements, and you feel you are learning more. This is not true. If you explore an unusual place and learn about their challenges and their way of doing things, it will hold maximum learning for you.

I was fortunate to be part of the Common Purpose Program for six months. It provided a very different perspective of looking at life. First of all, the group that was formed was a mix of people from the corporate, government, and NGO. If we are in the corporate world, we get news about government or NGO work through a media, newspaper, TV, etc. It was an eye-opener for me when I was grouped with these people for the first time. I realized that the people from the NGOs and government have their own perspective and they were also trying to see what best they could do to improve the society, but they have their own challenges. Working in this group gave me a lot of insights, looking at things from others' viewpoint, breaking the perceptions we had, and learning about the dimensions different organizations operate in.

The uniqueness of the program was also from the fact that every week we used to go to an unusual place. The places we visited included a hospital, a blind home, hospice care, a transportation hub, a government school, and many such unusual places. We got to meet people from different professions, learn about their challenges and their personal life.

All this taught me a valuable lesson. The world is big, and we are so constricted in our own worlds that we hardly open up to look beyond our work, family, and friends.

Associate yourself with a NON-Profit Organization:

Again here, I am extremely fortunate to be associated with the International Organization "Words of Peace" that promotes the message of bringing Peace in your life, through its founder and International Speaker Mr. Prem Rawat.

When you work for a cause without monetary benefit or any peer pressure, on your own time and dime, life teaches you to work as a team for a common goal. You can learn how you can lead without authority, and how your position changes based on tasks. In fact, everyone from the CXO level to the junior most employee in a corporate context when working for a good cause works with a very down to earth attitude. This teaches us humbleness, allows us to stay put on the ground, and do work entirely without any expectations. The result is pure happiness that comes from within. I still remember working together for days and nights, but there was nothing called stress.

> *Someone rightly said, "Stress is the GAP between the desired Ambition and your actual Performance". Pause and ponder over this sentence, it is very powerful statement.*

In corporate or business scenario, while running the rat race, it is most likely your ambitions are higher than your actual performance, which results in stress and unhealthy life. But when you work as a volunteer, your performance is much higher than your ambitions, leading to true fulfillment and it leads to enjoyment. The more your performance matches the ambitions you have, the more you will enjoy your work and life. Hence again, as you chase big aspirations, have small, short-term goals that you keep on achieving, it helps in keeping you on track towards your large ambitions/vision/goals.

Get a Personal Coach

It's important to see if you can get a coach. Don't confuse this with mentorship that is offered in most corporates and business today. Mentorship onus is always with the mentee, and it's not an oversight provided by a mentor. It is someone high up the ladder that can guide or provide an approach, or answer your query, etc.

In contrast, a coach is a person who guides you on every path, reviews your actions, points mistakes, allow you to think beyond, stretches you to the extreme to get the best out of you.

React vs. Response

There is a huge difference between reacting and responding. A reaction is typically quick, without much thought, tense and aggressive. A response is thought out, calm and non-threatening. A reaction typically provokes more reactions – perpetuating a long line of hatefulness with nothing accomplished. A response typically provokes discussion – perpetuating healthy discussion (debate even) that leads to resolution.

- The reaction is quick. Response takes time.
- The reaction is emotion-filled. Response removes all emotion.
- The reaction is often aggressive. Response allows for assertiveness without aggression.
- Reaction snowballs into unnecessary and prolonged periods of discontent and disagreement.
- Response resolves conflict quickly.

Story : React V/S Response

One evening during a nice party get-together at an ambient hotel, a cockroach flew from somewhere and sat on one of the ladies. She started screaming out of fear. With a panic-stricken face and trembling voice, she started jumping, desperately trying to get rid of the cockroach. Her reaction was contagious, everyone in her group got cranky. The lady finally managed to push the cockroach onto another lady in the group. Now, it was the turn of the other lady in the group to continue the drama. The waitress rushed forward to their rescue. In the relay of throwing, the cockroach fell on the waitress. She stood firm, composed herself and observed the behavior of the cockroach on her dress. When she was confident enough, she grabbed and threw it out with her fingers.

 More than the problem, it's your reaction to the problem that hurts you.

It is not the cockroach but the inability of the person to handle the disturbance caused by the cockroach.

You will realize this in life as well. It is not the shouting of your father or your boss that disturbs you, but it is your inability to handle the disturbances caused by their shouting that disturbs you.

It's not the traffic jams on the road that disturbs you but your inability to handle the disturbance caused by the traffic jam that disturbs you. Remember that you have to drive to your purpose.

> *You should always respond and not react to situations. Reactions are always instinctive whereas responses are always intellectual.*

Success vs. Satisfaction

Success is what others see depending on the goals that you have achieved. Satisfaction is the inner feeling of contentment. Sometimes even during a failure, the world would see that as a failure, while your internal soul depending on the efforts you have put in, can still be content and satisfied. Focus on achieving satisfaction. Despite failures, you will not lose hope and success will touch your feet.

 Success is always a measure or a comparison, while satisfaction is your own self content.

The Villager and the Happy Man
By Remez Sasson

In a small village in a valley, there lived a man who was always happy, kind, and well-disposed to everyone he met. He always smiled and had kind and encouraging words to say. Everyone that met him left feeling better, happier and elated. People knew they could count on him, and regarded him as a great friend.

One of the village dwellers was curious to know what his secret was, and how he could also be so kind and helpful. He wondered how is it that he held no grudge toward anyone and always was happy.

Once, upon meeting him in the street, he asked him:

"Most people are selfish and unsatisfied. They do not smile as often as you do, neither are they as helpful or kind as you are. How do you explain this?"

The man smiled at him and replied, "When you make peace with yourself, you can be at peace with the rest of the world. If you can recognize the spirit in yourself, you can recognize the spirit in everyone, and then you find it natural to be kind and well-disposed to all."

"If your thoughts are under your control, you become strong and firm.

The personality is like a robot programmed to do certain tasks. Your habits and thoughts are the tools and programs that control your personality. Become free from being programmed, and then, the inner good and the happiness that resides within you will be revealed."

"But a lot of work is necessary. Good habits have to be developed. The ability to concentrate and to control the thoughts has to be strengthened. The work is difficult and endless. There are many walls that need to be climbed. It is not an easy task." lamented the villager.

"Do not think about the difficulties otherwise this is what you will see and experience. Just quieten your feelings and thoughts and try to stay in this peace. Just try to be calm, and do not let yourself be carried away by your thoughts."

"Is that all?." asked the villager.

"Try to watch your thoughts and see how they come and go. Stay in the quietness that arises. The moments of peace will be brief at first, but in time they will get longer. This peace is also strength, power, kindness, and love. In time, you will realize that you are one with the Universal Power, and this will lead you to act from a different dimension – a point of view - consciousness, not from the selfish, small, limited ego."

"I will try to remember your words," said the villager and continued, "There is another thing that I am curious about. You do not seem to be influenced by the environment. You have a kind word for everyone, and you are helpful. People treat you well and never exploit your goodness."

"Being good and being kind does not necessarily point to weakness. When you are good, you can also be strong. People sense your inner strength, and therefore, do not impose on you. When you are strong and calm inside, you help people, because you can, and you want to. You act from strength, not from weakness. Goodness is not a sign of weakness, as some people erroneously think. It can manifest together with power and strength."

"Thank you very much for your advice and explanations." said the villager and went away happy and satisfied.

Your health is wealth.

The key aspect of your development is maintaining your health.

During my MindTree days, I was fortunate to be one of the few chosen seeds, who got a chance to receive personal coaching from the GARDENER Mr. Subroto Bagchi. I still remember the first meet we had. I went prepared with a lot of details on my career, what I wanted to achieve, my goals, my complaints, my suggestions, ideas, etc. As I entered the room, Subroto had my complete report card with him. To my surprise, he started with my health record; he said that my cholesterol was high. I was shocked and stranded. Then he went on to give me three pieces of advice:

1) Drink lots of water,
2) Stop the intake of sugar, mainly get rid of tea/coffee,
3) Change to olive oil. His advice was to get your fitness right in order to become a high achiever.

Though we went on for a nine months' cycle, doing many case studies, introspection, etc., and trying to find my interventions and purpose, this first meet has found a permanent place in my memory.

Your health and fitness provide you with a very high level of self-confidence. It displays that charm on your face. It gives your words a power to speak and gives your actions the power to create an impact.

Being Mindful

Being mindful is about being in the moment. Not worrying about the past and not worrying about your future. Although you are marching towards your purpose with a well laid out vision for yourself, it's important that you enjoy the journey and not the goal post itself. Being in the present allows you to look at things and opportunities as they come to you, enabling you to do the right thing without any biases.

Story: The Elephant Rope – Use your power and believe in yourself. [2]

Ever wondered why a huge elephant is not able to use his powers to break a small rope that he is attached to?

---

[2]Source: https://wealthygorilla.com/10-most-inspirational-short-stories/

A gentleman was walking through an elephant camp. He

noticed that the elephants weren't being kept in cages or held by the use of chains. All that was holding them back from escaping was a small piece of rope tied to one of their legs.

As the man gazed at the elephants, he was completely confused wondering why the elephants didn't use their strength to break the rope and escape the camp. They could have easily done so, but they didn't try to at all.

Curious and wanting to know the answer, he asked a trainer nearby why the elephants never tried to escape.

The trainer replied:

"When they are very young and much smaller we use the same size rope to tie them and, at that age, it's enough to hold them. As they grow up, they are conditioned to believe they cannot break away. They believe the rope can still hold them, so they never try to break free."

The only reason that the elephants weren't breaking free and escaping from the camp was that over time they came to believe that it just wasn't possible.

No matter how much the world tries to hold you back, always continue with the belief that what, you want to achieve is possible.

 Believing in yourself is the most important step in actually achieving it.

Story: The King and his 4 Wives

Once upon a time, there was a rich king who had four wives.

He loved the 4th wife the most. He gave her rich robes and treated her to the finest of delicacies. He gave her nothing but the best.

He also loved the 3rd wife very much and was always showing her off to neighboring kingdoms. However, he feared that one day she would leave him for another.

He also loved his 2nd wife. She was his confidant and was always kind, considerate and patient with him. Whenever the king faced a problem, he could confide in her, and she would help him get through the difficult times.

The king's 1st wife was a very loyal partner and had made great contributions in maintaining his wealth and kingdom. However, he did not love the first wife. Although she loved him deeply, he hardly took notice of her.

One day, the King fell ill, and he knew his time was short.

He thought of his luxurious life and wondered, "I have four wives with me right now, but when I die, I'll be all alone."

Thus, he said to his 4th wife, "I loved you the most, endowed you with the finest clothing and showered great care over you. Now that I'm dying, will you follow me and keep me company?"

"No way!." replied the 4th wife, and she walked away without another word.

Her answer cut like a sharp knife right into his heart.

The sad king then asked the 3rd wife, "I loved you all my life. Now that I'm dying, will you follow me and keep me company?"

"No!." replied the 3rd wife. "Life is too good! When you die, I'm going to remarry!"

His heart sank and turned cold.

He then asked the 2nd wife, "I have always turned to you for help, and you've always been there for me.

When I die, will you follow me and keep me company?"

"I'm sorry, I can't help you out this time!." replied the 2nd wife. "At the very most, I can only walk with you to your grave."

Her answer struck him like a bolt of lightning, and the king was devastated. Then a voice called out: "I'll go with you. I'll follow you no matter where you go."

The king looked up and there she was, his first wife. She was very skinny as she suffered from malnutrition and neglect.

Greatly grieved, the king said, "I should have taken much better care of you when I had the chance!"

In truth, we all have the 4 wives in our lives:

Our 4th wife is our body. No matter how much time and effort we lavish in making it look good, it will leave us when we die.

Our 3rd wife is our possessions, status and wealth. When we die, it will go to others.

Our 2nd wife is our family and friends. No matter how much they have been there for us, the farthest they can stay by us is up to the grave.

And our 1st wife is our soul. Often neglected in pursuit of wealth, power pleasures of the world.

However, our soul is the only thing that will follow us wherever we go. Cultivate, strengthen and cherish it now, for it is the only part of us that will follow and continue with us throughout eternity.

Hope that you now have an understanding of Development, and how you can use your learnings towards complete development of the mind, body, and soul.

Note down your learning in the below template. Identify your current state and your desired state, so that you can come up with an action plan to build a foundation of Development in your life.

EXCERSICE 6: DEVELOPMENT

List down your current state of Development, desired state and the actions you will take to move from current state to desired state

CURRENT STATE

_____

_____

_____

_____

DESIRED STATE

_____

_____

_____

_____

ACTIONS

_____

_____

_____

7

EXCELLENCE

Excellence is Never an ACCIDENT; It is always the result of HIGH INTENTION, SINCERE EFFORTS, INTELLIGENT EXECUTION; it represents the WISE choice of many alternatives - CHOICE, NOT CHANCE, determines your DESTINY.
— ARISTOTLE

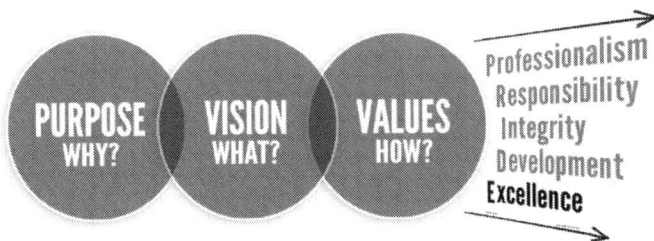

Striving for excellence means commitment, a passion and continued effort to succeed. Excellence does not come with mediocrity. It does not come with a daily routine of 9 AM to 5 PM, but in fact, requires you to put yourself in command of your own life.

You have one lifetime and 30% of the time is consumed as part of your sleep and rest. If you want to bring out a life that you are truly proud of, you need to have the qualities to excel. Excellence is going that extra mile and not giving up when you are close.

The 3 Ps for Excellence:

Passion – A strong feeling of enthusiasm or excitement for something or about doing something

Persistence - Continuing firmly or obstinately in an opinion or course of action in spite of opposition or challenges.

Perseverance – Persistence in doing something despite difficulty or delay in achieving success

It's important to note that the road to excellence is not easy. It is a commitment that you make to yourself, to overcome challenges and obstacles, and clear the way to reach your goal.

> *Remember: It is also not about merely reaching your goal but getting there with very strong confidence, the pleasure of fighting the odds, and the content feeling of being there once you reach the post.*

Simple ways to thrive in excellence:

- THINK Positive – half full not half empty
- THINK Solutions – not problems
- THINK Big Picture – not small tasks
- THINK Opportunities – not challenges
- THINK Business Goals – not technologies
- THINK Customer – not problems
- THINK Automation – not mundane tasks
- THINK Collaborations – not silos
- THINK Alternatives – not one approach
- THINK out-of-the-box – not within boundaries
- THINK Simplicity – not complexity
- THINK to Experience – not always a success
- THINK Present – not past or future

Challenges vs. Opportunities – 2 sides of the same coin.

In ancient times, a king had a boulder placed on a roadway. He then hid and watched to see if anyone would move the rock out of the way. Some of the king's wealthiest merchants and courtiers came by and simply walked around it.

Many people loudly blamed the king for not keeping the roads clear but none of them did anything to get the stone out of the way.

A peasant then came along carrying a load of vegetables. Upon approaching the boulder, the peasant laid down his burden and tried to push the stone out of the road. After much pushing and straining, he finally succeeded.

After the peasant went back to pick up his vegetables, he noticed a purse lying on the road where the boulder had been. The purse contained many gold coins and a note from the king explaining that the gold was for the person who removed the boulder from the roadway.

Every obstacle we come across in life is not a challenge but a hidden opportunity to either improve yourself or some bigger things that could unfold. While the lazy complain about challenges they face, the achievers are creating opportunities from the same challenges through their kind hearts, generosity, and willingness to get things done.

Remember: Our struggles in life develop our strengths and self-confidence.

Develop networks and relationships

In an increasingly social world, we are always on and always connected. This is the best phase of your life, where you have the opportunity to get more people associated with your purpose. Networks are the best way to increase your reach and for you to be known as part of a broader community. Being linked to a professional network is an excellent way to connect with like-minded people and professionals.

It's also good to use LinkedIn and Twitter (with relevant feeds) to get the inspiration, knowledge, and linkage to people who can help you move forward. Post your queries or point of views on such platforms, share your experience and insights so that others can share their perspectives as well. All networks lead to relationships. We human beings are social creatures, and we love being in a community. The more the relationships, contributing to your personal life in some way, the better life you will live for yourself.

Self-review and feedback

As you move towards your purpose and start looking at

achieving your goals/vision, it is important to have regular self-governance. You must review and provide self-feedback for what you have accomplished thus far.

A general review of your short terms goals on a monthly basis along with an analysis of your purpose and associated long-term goals on a quarterly basis is the best way to keep yourself updated on your progress. It is a good way to know if a change in direction or if some elements of your ultimate vision needs to be relooked. If you feel that something is unachievable, it is always better to break that into smaller goals.

Try things above your ability and set high goals. You might be pleasantly surprised to know how you are progressing. Always aim high and success will follow.

It's important not to give up, change your goals or divide your goals and focus on achieving them. The moment you get distracted from your goals, there are high chances of you giving up, so stay on course.

Pen it down:

When striving for excellence, it is important to focus on the tasks you do. Remember, the to-do list we talked during self-development, it is essential to pen it down.

Once you have a to-do list and you look at your tasks, you may choose to ignore some, where the effort is high, but the value is very less. A simple example is picking up a relative from an airport. If the airport is 50 miles away, it will take you a couple of hours to reach, wait there and then come back; you will waste almost half a day. Instead of putting your time and energy on things that are of a lesser value, you may choose to book a taxi for them and when the relative comes home, spend that time with them. It seems simple, but once you start putting a value on the tasks, you will start focusing on things that are of higher value and dropping the ones with lesser value.

Excellence in Teams

If you are part of a team, the following actions may help:

Use a common action task plan that is shared with your team. You or anyone on the team should spend the least time in doing a follow-up. So once the tasks are assigned, owner and date are published, it should become the responsibility of the owner to update the status on task and seek help or guidance as needed. This saves a lot of time for the entire team. People take their responsibility for their actions and hence, the team becomes highly productive.

Celebrate Together – Every small milestone, or completion of intermediate projects, requires celebration. It's a recognition of the hard work put in by the team, and once you celebrate together beyond emails and flashes, it increases the team bonding and allows the team to work with each other cordially.

Question the Status-QUO – Be the change catalyst

In a team situation, when you get to a state where nothing seems to be moving, and no one is coming forward, take responsibility and be the change catalyst. Bring in a new dimension or a project that would rejuvenate the team and keep them motivated. Changes are difficult, but this becomes a good opportunity for you to take the situation at hand and emerge as a possible leader. Don't allow yourself to be dragged in such a status-QUO but rise to the occasion and make the best use of it.

Work Business Backward - Customer First

When in doubt about the approaches, always give the customer priority. Note that the customer may not be always right, but he has to win. Business is about customers, and strong team or organization values towards the customer will make the business flourish. Repeat business is the measure of a highly satisfied customer, and repeat business drops your sales cost considerably. The repeat business also turns your customers into promoters, and they would be eager to provide a reference for a new customer, hence helping you grow your business.

Appreciation – Rewards and Recognitions

As you start holding people responsible and accountable, you need to go all the way to sincerely reward and appreciate the team and individuals on a continuing basis, especially when driving towards team excellence. Rewards have a snowball effect and get the slow runners motivated and get the high performers to put in more effort. This helps in increasing the total productivity of your team output.

Identify, manage and take calculated risks.

Every change comes with associated risks. The risk is critical because, without it, you would not push yourself or your team's boundaries, never realizing your real potential. Hence, be open to taking risks and trying different ways to handle the problem. Every risk has a downside as well. Thus, a calculated risk is the best way to go. The way to do a calculated risk would mean putting a probability value of the occurrence of the risk and weighing the benefits of it over the possible losses.

Leadership Excellence: (For Leaders)

Leadership excellence involves focusing on the customers' needs, keeping the employees confident and empowered, and continually improving the current activities in the workplace.

The STOP Tool [3]

The unconscious activity of performance momentum is succinctly satirized in the lyrics of "I'm in a Hurry," made famous by the band Alabama in the early nineties.

"I'm in a hurry to get things done. Oh, I rush and rush until life's no fun. All I got to do is live and die. But I'm in a hurry and don't know why."

STOP-START-STOP—How many times in a single workday do you have to interrupt what you are doing to start something else? You may even stop something important to take care of a time-sensitive but less important task. In my workday, there can easily be more than twenty such "interruptions." If I'm in my self-performance momentum, each interruption brings an automatic reaction of annoyance and with it a loss of conscious mobility.

The alternative is first to stop and make a conscious choice about if and when to interrupt what you are doing. This stop doesn't take away the consequences of the interruption. But allows me to exercise my choice which removes the annoyance and provides a sense of freedom and enjoyment because I still have my hands on the steering wheel of my work day.

---

[3] Credit: The Inner Game by Timothy Gallwey

If I decide yes, then before starting the new activity, I take a short stop to consciously "close the books" on the last activity and to orient myself to the purpose and context of the next.

Creating a sense of closure on each activity and making a conscious choice about the next, relieves the mind from carrying an accumulating burden of unfinished tasks.

It can make all the difference between a satisfying day of deliberate choices and what otherwise could feel like a fatiguing day of unnecessary interruptions.

The trick is to realize that you don't have to carry unfinished tasks in your mind; you can lay them down, knowing they will be there when you have the chance to pick them up again.

Here are just a few of the benefits of practicing Stop-Start-Stop:

- More acknowledgment of work accomplished
- Lesser work burden carried home at the end of the day
- More conscious choices made
- Feeling more rested and energized during and after work
- More innovation available
A more precise sense of purpose and priority
- More conscious changes made where needed
- Remembering one's learning goal
- Checking on feeling levels – enjoyment, stress, tiredness
- Remembering forgotten commitments
- Deciding whether a more prolonged stop is needed

The benefits are many. But the key to doing this as a Habit

comes only with Discipline. But once you make this tool as a habit, you will excel in your life journey.

An approach to problem-solving

Once you become good at problem-solving, you are driving towards your excellence.

Below are the steps you could take to be a great problem solver:

- Define the problem
- Use the 'Why' query to deep dive into the cause of the problem
- Collect as much data as possible (without judgment)
- Structure the problem or break into different groups
- Identify options and approaches to solve the problem
- Weigh your options and determine a value for each of the approaches
- Get inputs from your environment (people, friend, team, etc.)
- Select the best option and proceed
- Review timely and see if the option is helping you move forward. If yes, continue and refine the approach with more data.
- Else, relook at options again and select the next best, until you find the best possible option which provides the greatest value.

Story: A Beautiful Solution

A father was engrossed in his work while his little daughter constantly distracted him in an attempt to make him play with her. To keep her busy, the man tore a page of the printed map of the world from a magazine into pieces and asked her to go to her room and put them back together to make the map again. The daughter was very young, and he was pretty sure that she would take hours to get it done.

The father was surprised when he saw his little one coming out of the room with a smile and the perfect map within a few minutes. The stunned man asked his daughter how she could solve the puzzle quickly.

"Daddy, there is a woman's face on the other side of the paper, When I made a face perfect, I got the map right.." replied the young girl.

Remember: There is always another side to whatever you experience in this world. Whenever you come across a challenge or a puzzling situation, look at the other side. You will be surprised to see a different approach to tackle the problem.

"We cannot solve the problems with the same thinking we used when we created them" – Albert Einstein.

Excel for Yourself and Not for Others

Don't climb a mountain with an intention that the world should see you, climb the mountain with an intention to see the world.

A German once visited a temple that was under construction. He saw a sculptor making an idol of God.

Suddenly he saw a similar idol lying nearby. Surprised, he asked the sculptor, "Do you need two statues of the same idol?"

"No," said the sculptor without looking up, "We need

only one, but the first one got damaged at the last stage."

The gentleman examined the idol but did not find any apparent damage. "Where is the damage?" he asked.

"There is a scratch on the nose of the idol." said the sculptor still busy with his work.

"Where are you going to install the idol?"

The sculptor replied that it would be installed on a pillar that is 20-feet high.

"If the idol is that far up, who is going to know that there is a scratch on the nose?" the gentleman asked.

The sculptor stopped his work, looked up at the gentleman, smiled and said, "I will know it.".

Remember: The desire to excel is exclusive of the fact whether someone appreciates it or not.

Excellence is a drive from the inside not outside. It is not for someone else to notice but for your satisfaction and efficiency.

Hope that you have an understanding of Excellence and know how you can use your learnings for your development.

Note down your learning in the below template. Identify your current state and your desired state, so that you can come up with an action plan to build a foundation of Excellence in your life.

List down your current state of excellence, desired state and the actions you will take to move from current state to the desired state.

Note that if you are working in the team you can put together the same template for team excellence, and

If you are a leader, you can put the same template as the leadership excellence.

EXERCISE 7 : EXCELLENCE

CURRENT STATE

_____

_____

_____

_____

DESIRED STATE

_____

_____

_____

ACTIONS

_____

_____

_____

_____

8

INSPIRATIONAL LIFE STORIES OF GREAT PEOPLE

Here, I shall talk about a few life journeys of our century that will guide and inspire you to create your own life story. [4]

Here are the four great people I admire; I believe you will also learn a lot about Purpose, Vision and P.R.I.D.E Values from these stories

- AZIZ PREMJI – founder WIPRO
- STEVE JOBS – founder APPLE
- JACK MA – founder ALIBABA
- JEFF BEZOS– founder AMAZON

Source : Publicly published data from the internet.

AZIZ PREMJI[4]

If people are not laughing at your goals, your goals are too small - Azim Premji

Azim Hashim Premji (born 24 July 1945) is an Indian business tycoon, investor, and philanthropist, who is the chairman of Wipro Limited. He is informally known as the Czar of the Indian IT Industry. He was responsible for guiding Wipro through four decades of diversification and growth to finally emerge as one of the global leaders in the software industry. In 2010, he was voted among the 20 most powerful men in the world by Asiaweek. He has twice been listed among the 100 most influential people by TIME Magazine, once in 2004 and more recently in 2011.

He is currently the second richest person in India with an estimated net worth of US$19.5 billion as of November 2017. In 2013, he agreed to give away at least half of his wealth by signing The Giving Pledge. Premji started with a $2.2 billion donation to the Azim Premji Foundation, focused on education in India.

Premji was born in Bombay, India in a Nizari Ismaili Shia Muslim family with origins from Kutch in Gujarat. His father was a noted businessman and was known as *Rice King of Burma*. After partition, when Jinnah invited his father Muhammed Hashem Premji to come to Pakistan, he turned down the request and chose to remain in India.

Premji has a Bachelor of Science in Electrical Engineering degree (equivalent to a Bachelor of Engineering degree) from Stanford University, USA. He is married to Yasmeen. The couple have two children, Rishad and Tariq. Rishad is currently the Chief Strategy Officer of IT Business, Wipro.

n 1945, Muhammed Hashim Premji incorporated Western

Indian Vegetable Products Ltd, based at Amalner, a small town in the Jalgaon district of Maharashtra. It used to manufacture cooking oil under the brand name Sunflower Vanaspati, and a laundry soap called 787, a by-product of oil manufacture. In 1966, on the news of his father's death, the then 21-year-old Azim Premji returned home from Stanford University, where he was studying engineering, to take charge of Wipro. The company, which was called Western Indian Vegetable Products at the time, dealt in hydrogenated oil manufacturing but Azim Premji later diversified the company to bakery fats, ethnic ingredient based toiletries, hair care soaps, baby toiletries, lighting products, and hydraulic cylinders. In the 1980s, the young entrepreneur, recognising the importance of the emerging IT field, took advantage of the vacuum left behind by the expulsion of IBM from India, changed the company name to *Wipro* and entered the high-technology sector by manufacturing minicomputers under technological collaboration with an American company Sentinel Computer Corporation. Thereafter Premji made a focused shift from soaps to software. [PURPOSE]

In 2001, he founded Azim Premji Foundation, a non-profit organisation, with a vision to significantly contribute to achieving quality universal education that facilitates a just, equitable, humane and sustainable society. The works in the area of elementary education to pilot and develop 'proofs of concept' that have a potential for systemic change in India's 1.3 million government-run schools. A specific focus is on working in rural areas where the majority of these schools exist. This choice to work with elementary education (Class I to VIII) in rural government-run is a response to evidence of educational attainment in India.

The non-profit organisation set up by Premji in 2001 currently functions across Karnataka, Uttarakhand, Rajasthan, Chhattisgarh, Puducherry, Andhra Pradesh, Bihar and Madhya Pradesh, in close partnership with various state governments. The foundation has worked largely in rural areas, to help contribute to the improvement of quality and equity of school education.

In December 2010, he pledged to donate US$2 billion for improving school education in India. This has been done by transferring 213 million equity shares of Wipro Ltd, held by a few entities controlled by him, to the Azim Premji Trust. This donation is the largest of its kind in India.

Premji has said that being rich "did not thrill" him. He became the first Indian to sign up for The Giving Pledge, a campaign led by Warren Buffett and Bill Gates, to encourage the wealthiest people to make a commitment to give most of their wealth to philanthropic causes. He is the third non-American after Richard Branson and David Sainsbury to join this philanthropy club.

"I strongly believe that those of us, who are privileged to have wealth, should contribute significantly to try and create a better world for the millions who are far less privileged"--- Azim Premji

Premji has been recognised by Business Week as one of the *Greatest Entrepreneurs* for being responsible for Wipro emerging as one of the world's fastest growing companies.

In 2000, he was conferred an honorary doctorate by the Manipal Academy of Higher Education. In 2006, Azim Premji was awarded Lakshya Business Visionary by National Institute of Industrial Engineering, Mumbai. In 2009, he was awarded an honorary doctorate from Wesleyan University in Middletown, Connecticut for his outstanding philanthropic work. In 2015, Mysore University conferred an honorary doctorate on him.

- In 2005, the Government of India honoured him with the title of Padma Bhushan for his outstanding work in trade and commerce.

- In 2011, he has been awarded Padma Vibhushan, the second highest civilian award by the Government of India.

- In 2013, he received the ET Lifetime Achievement Award.

- In 2015, University of Mysore conferred the honorary doctorate to Azim Premji.

- In April 2017, India Today magazine ranked him 9th in India's 50 Most powerful people of 2017 list.

"I was 21 and had spent the last few years in Stanford University Engineering School at California. Many people advised me to take up a nice, cushy job rather than face the challenges of running a hydrogenated oil business. Looking back, I am glad I decided to take charge instead. Essentially leadership begins from within. It is a small voice that tells you where to go when you feel lost. If you believe in that voice, you believe in yourself." – Azim Premji

---

[4] Source – Azim Premji - https://en.wikipedia.org/wiki/Azim_Premji

STEVE JOBS[5]

Steve Jobs, the American businessman and technology visionary who is best known as the co-founder, chairman, and chief executive officer of Apple Inc., was born on February 24, 1955. His parents were two University of Wisconsin graduate students, Joanne Carole Schieble and Syrian-born Abdulfattah Jandali.

The Jobs family moved from San Francisco to Mountain View, California when Steve was five years old. The parents later adopted a daughter, Patti. Paul was a machinist for a company that made lasers and taught his son rudimentary electronics and how to work with his hands. The father showed Steve how to work on electronics in the family garage, demonstrating to his son how to take apart and rebuild electronics such as radios and televisions. As a result, Steve became interested in and developed a hobby of technical tinkering. Clara was an accountant who taught him to read before he went to school.

Jobs then attended Cupertino Junior High and Homestead High School in Cupertino, California. During the following years, Jobs met Bill Fernandez and Steve Wozniak, a computer whiz kid.

Following high school graduation in 1972, Jobs enrolled at Reed College in Portland, Oregon. Reed was an expensive college which Paul and Clara could ill afford. They were spending much of their life savings on their son's higher education. Jobs dropped out of college after six months and spent the next 18 months dropping in on creative classes, including a course on calligraphy. He continued auditing classes at Reed while sleeping on the floor in friends' dorm rooms, returning Coke bottles for food money, and getting weekly free meals at the local Hare Krishna temple.

In 1976, Wozniak invented the Apple I computer. Jobs, Wozniak, and Ronald Wayne, an electronics industry worker, founded Apple computer in the garage of Jobs' parents to sell it. They received funding from a then-semi-retired Intel product-marketing manager and engineer Mike Markkula.

Through Apple, Jobs was widely recognized as a charismatic pioneer of the personal computer revolution and for his influential career in the computer and consumer electronics fields. Jobs also co-founded and served as chief executive of Pixar Animation Studios; he became a member of the board of directors of The Walt Disney Company in 2006 when Disney acquired Pixar.

Jobs died at his California home around 3 PM on October 5, 2011, due to complications from a relapse of his previously treated pancreatic cancer.

Steve said, "In 1984, Apple introduced the first Macintosh. It didn't change Apple. It changed the whole computer industry. In 2001, we introduced the first iPod. It didn't change the way we all listen to music. It changed the entire music industry."

In 2007, Apple successfully entered the mobile phone market, with the iPhone. This had features of the iPod, offering a multi-functional and touch screen device that became one of the best-selling electronic products. In 2010, he introduced the iPad – a revolutionary new style of tablet computers.

The design philosophy of Steve Jobs was to start with a fresh slate and imagine a new product that people would want to use. This contrasted with the alternative approach of trying to adapt current models to consumer feedback and focus groups. Job's explains his philosophy of innovative design, "But in the end, for something this complicated, it's really hard to design products by focus groups. A lot of times, people don't know what they want until you show it to them."

[5] Source : Steve Jobs, Business Week (25th May 1998)

JACK MA – FOUNDER ALIBABA [6]

Ma Yun born September 10, 1964, known professionally as Jack Ma, is a Chinese business magnate, investor, and philanthropist. He is the co-founder and executive chairman of the Alibaba Group, a multinational technology conglomerate. As of February 2018, he is one of China's richest men with a net worth of US$41.3 billion, as well as one of the wealthiest people in the world.

Ma was born on 10 September 1964 in Hangzhou, Zhejiang, China. He began studying English at a young age by conversing with English-speakers at Hangzhou international hotel. He would ride 70 miles on his bicycle to give tourists tours of the area to practice his English for nine years. He became pen pals with one of those foreigners, who nicknamed him "Jack" because he found it hard to pronounce his Chinese name.

Jack Ma applied for 30 different jobs and got rejected by all. "I went for a job with the police, they said, 'you're no good,'" Ma told interviewer Charlie Rose. "I even went to KFC when it came to my city. Twenty-four people went for the job. Twenty-three were accepted. I was the only guy". He applied to Harvardt en times and got rejected.

In 1994, Ma heard about the Internet. In early 1995, he went to the US, his friends, helped him get introduced to the Internet. During his first encounter, he searched the word "beer". Although he found information related to beer from many countries, he was surprised to find none from China. Further, he tried to search for general information about China and again was surprised to find none. So, he and his friend created an "ugly" website related to China. He launched the website at 9:40 AM, and by 12:30 PM he had received emails from some Chinese, wishing to know about him. This was when Ma realized that the Internet had something great to offer. In April 1995, Ma, his wife, and a friend raised US$ 20,000 and started their first company. Their company was dedicated to creating websites for companies. He named their company "China Yellow Pages." Within three years, his company had made 5,000,000 Chinese Yuan which was equivalent to US$800,000.

Ma began building websites for Chinese companies with the help of friends in the US. He has said that "the day we got connected to the web, I invited friends and TV people over to my house," and on a very slow dial-up connection, "we waited three and a half hours and got half a page.... We drank, watched TV and played cards, waiting. But I was so proud. I proved (to my house guests that) the Internet existed." At a conference in 2010, Ma revealed that he has never actually written a line of code nor made one sale to a customer. He acquired a computer for the first time at the age of 33.

From 1998 to 1999, Ma headed an information technology company established by the China International Electronic Commerce Center, a department of the Ministry of Foreign Trade and Economic Cooperation. In 1999, he quit and returned to Hangzhou with his team to found Alibaba, a China-based business-to-business marketplace site in his apartment with a group of 18 friends. He started a new round of venture development with 500,000 yuan

In October 1999 and January 2000, Alibaba won a total of a $25 million foreign venture capital investment twice. The program was expected to improve the domestic e-commerce market and perfect an e-commerce platform for Chinese enterprises, especially small and medium-sized enterprises (SMEs), to address World Trade Organization (WTO) challenges. Ma wanted to improve the global e-commerce system, and from 2003 he founded Taobao Marketplace, Alipay, Ali Mama, and Lynx. After the rapid rise of Taobao, eBay offered to purchase the company. However, Ma rejected their offer, instead garnering support from Yahoo co-founder Jerry Yang with a $1 billion investment.

In September 2014, it was reported Alibaba was raising over $25 billion in an initial public offering (IPO) on the New York Stock Exchange. [18]Alibaba became one of the most valuable tech companies in the world after raising $25 billion, the largest initial public offering in US financial history. Ma now serves as executive chairman of Alibaba Group, which is a holding company with nine major subsidiaries: Alibaba.com, Taobao Marketplace, Tmall, eTao, Alibaba Cloud Computing, Juhuasuan, 1688.com, AliExpress.com, and Alipay. In November 2012, Alibaba's online transaction volume exceeded one trillion yuan. Ma has often been invited to lecture at universities such as the Wharton School at the University of Pennsylvania, Massachusetts Institute of Technology, Harvard University, and Peking University. [19] As of 2016, Ma is the owner of Château de Sours in Bordeaux, Chateau Guerry in Côtes de Bourg and Château Perenne in Blaye, Côtes de Bordeaux.

Success and profitability are outcomes of focusing on customers and employees, not objectives – Jack Ma, founder Alibaba.

In September 2018, Jack Ma, said he planned to step down from the Chinese e-commerce giant Alibaba to pursue philanthropy in education.

---

[6] Source : https://en.wikipedia.org/wiki/Jack_Ma

JEFF BEZOS – FOUNDER AMAZON[7]

Entrepreneur and e-commerce pioneer Jeff Bezos was born on January 12, 1964, in Albuquerque, New Mexico. Bezos had an early love of computers and studied computer science and electrical engineering at Princeton University. After graduation, he worked on Wall Street, and in 1990 he became the youngest senior vice president at the investment firm D.E. Shaw. Four years later, he quit his lucrative job to open Amazon.com, a virtual bookstore that became one of the internet's biggest success stories. In 2013, Bezos purchased The Washington Post in a $250 million deal. His successful business ventures have made him one of the richest people in the world.

As a child, Jeff Bezos showed an early interest in how things work, turning his parents' garage into a laboratory and rigging electrical contraptions around his house. He moved to Miami with his family as a teenager, where he developed a love for computers and graduated valedictorian of his high school. It was during high school that he started his first business, the Dream Institute, an educational summer camp for fourth, fifth and sixth graders.

Bezos pursued his interest in computers at Princeton University, where he graduated from summa cum laude in 1986 with a degree in computer science and electrical engineering. After graduation, he found work at several firms on Wall Street, including Fitel, Bankers Trust, and the investment firm D.E. Shaw. During this tenure, he met his wife, Mackenzie, and became the company's youngest vice president in 1990.

While his career in finance was extremely lucrative, Bezos chose to make a risky move into the nascent world of e-commerce. He quit his job in 1994, moved to Seattle and targeted the untapped potential of the internet market by opening an online bookstore.

Bezos set up the office for his fledgling company in his garage where, along with a few employees, he began developing software. They expanded operations into a two-bedroom house, equipped with three Sun Microstations, and eventually developed a test site. After inviting 300 friends to beta test the site, Bezos opened Amazon.com, named after the meandering South American River, on July 16, 1995.

The initial success of the company was meteoric. With no press promotion, Amazon.com sold books across the United States and in 45 foreign countries within 30 days. In two months, sales reached $20,000 a week, growing faster than Bezos and his start-up team had envisioned.

Amazon.com went public in 1997, leading many market analysts to question whether the company could hold its own when traditional retailers launched their e-commerce sites. Two years later, the start-up not only kept up but also outpaced competitors, becoming an e-commerce leader.

Bezos continued to diversify Amazon's offerings with the sale of CDs and videos in 1998, and later clothes, electronics, toys and more through major retail partnerships. While many dot-coms of the early '90s went bust, Amazon flourished with yearly sales that jumped from $510,000 in 1995 to over $17 billion in 2011.

In 2006, Amazon.com launched its video on demand service; initially known as Amazon Unbox on TiVo; it was eventually rebranded as Amazon Instant Video. In 2007, the company released the Kindle, a handheld digital book reader that allowed users to buy, download, read and store their book selections. That same year, Bezos announced his investment in Blue Origin, a Seattle-based aerospace company that develops technologies to offer space travel to paying customers.

Bezos entered Amazon into the tablet marketplace with the unveiling of the Kindle Fire in 2011. The following September, he announced the new Kindle Fire HD, the company's next-generation tablet designed to give Apple's iPad a run for its money. "We haven't built the best tablet at a certain price. We have built the best tablet at any price," Bezos said, according to ABC News.

Bezos made headlines worldwide on August 5, 2013, when he purchased The Washington Post and other publications affiliated with its parent company, The Washington Post Co., for $250 million. The deal marked the end of the four-generation reign over The Post Co. by the Graham family, which included Donald E. Graham, the company's chairman and chief executive, and his niece, post publisher Katharine Weymouth.

In early December 2013, Bezos made headlines when he revealed a new, experimental initiative by Amazon, called "Amazon Prime Air," using drones—remote-controlled machines that can perform an array of human tasks—to provide delivery services to customers. According to Bezos, these drones can carry items weighing up to five pounds and are capable of traveling within a 10-mile distance of the company's distribution center. He also stated that Prime Air could become a reality within as little as four or five years.

Bezos oversaw one of Amazon's few major missteps when the company launched the Fire Phone in 2014; criticized for being too gimmicky, it was discontinued the following year. However, Bezos did score a victory with the development of original content through Amazon Studios. After premiering several new programs in 2013, Amazon hit it big in 2014 with the critically acclaimed Transparent and Mozart in the Jungle. In 2015, the company produced and released Spike Lee's Chi-

Raq as its first original feature film.

In July 2017, Bezos briefly surpassed Microsoft founder Bill Gates to become the richest person in the world, according to Bloomberg, before dropping back to No. 2. The Amazon chief then reclaimed the top spot in October, and in January 2018, Bloomberg pegged his net worth at $105.1 billion, making Bezos the richest person.

After going through these inspiring lives, go back to your purpose, vision and PRIDE values, and fine tune the same with these new learnings.

---

[7] Source : Publicly published data from the internet.

9

SUMMARIZE YOUR LEARNINGS
PURPOSE, VISION AND P.R.I.D.E VALUES

As it is rightly said, there are six ethics in life:

* Before you PRAY – BELIEVE
* Before you SPEAK – LISTEN
* Before you SPEND – EARN
* Before you WRITE – THINK
* Before you QUIT – TRY
* Before you DIE – LIVE

Taking action is about consolidating all the lessons learned into a single template. This template will help identify your purpose, your vision, and your PRIDE attributes that will build your attitude and character.

> *It's the capability or skills that takes you to the top, but it's your character that helps maintain your position while you are on top. Embrace simplicity and humility in your life and make the best use of this precious life that the almighty has blessed you with.*

Use the below template to summarize your learnings. Use this to identify, define and track your personal life and design a LIFE you desire, with a true purpose, clarity of vision, and foundational P.R.I.D.E values that will build a strong foundation for your life.

MY PERSONAL PURPOSE OF LIFE IS

_____

_____

_____

_____

_____

_____

MY PERSONAL VISION OF LIFE IS

- ■ _____
- ■ _____
- ■ _____
- ■ _____
- ■ _____
- ■ _____
- ■ _____
- ■ _____
- ■ _____

LONG TERM (aligned to PURPOSE)

_____

_____

_____

_____

_____

_____

MY SHORT TERM GOALs are (Typically 1-5 years depending on where you are in your LIFE)

_____

_____

_____

_____

_____

_____

ACTIONS to increase my **P.R.I.D.E** Values

PROFESSIONALISM

_____

_____

_____

_____

_____

RESPONSIBILITY

_____

_____

_____

_____

INTEGRITY

_____

_____

_____

_____

_____

SELF-DEVELOPMENT

_____

_____

_____

_____

_____

EXCELLENCE

_____

_____

_____

_____

10

LIVE YOUR P.R.I.D.E MOMENT

LIVE YOUR P.R.I.D.E MOMENT

The journey to excellence is not easy. It requires passion, commitment, hard work and actions (not mere words).

- If you want to be successful, start your journey NOW, not later
- Take time to understand yourself
- Don't accept failure in your Life
- Feel the gratitude and accept life how it is. Make the best use of this existence
- Don't get worried about what people will say, do what your heart desires (not what your mind wants).

Every day, enjoy this life, enjoy this existence. End each day with:

- How was my day today?
- Am I satisfied and happy?

- How much happiness has the brought me?
- Am I aligned with my purpose and vision?
- Am I reflecting and performing my best?

Now that you have understood the framework and made your own design template, you can go ahead and read the sections that can help you further. Make changes to the template, revise this template every week, and soon you will start seeing changes in your personal and professional LIFE.

Note that you can make a habit of any action you want to take. Make it a daily or weekly practice, and you will soon realize that this practice will, in a couple of months, turn into a habit. This could also mean behavioral changes you will bring to your life.

I strongly suggest to have a personal coach in your life. If you want any suggestions or clarity, please drop your message on https://www.pride-thebook.com, and I will be happy to discuss, and share my knowledge and experience with you.

Myth About "Why Me"

When faced with a crisis or challenging situation, you always think "why me." why is that almighty selected me for this problem?

Let me end this book with a beautiful message from Arthur Ashe. The legendary Wimbledon player, who was suffering from AIDS, which he contracted due to the infected blood he received during heart surgery in 1983.

During his illness, he received letters from his fans, one of which conveyed:

"Why did GOD have to select you for such a bad disease?"

To this Arthur Ashe replied:
- 50 million children started playing tennis
- 5 Million learned to play tennis
- 500,000 learned professional tennis
- 50,000 came to the circuit
- 5,000 reached a Grand Slam
- 50 reached Wimbledon
- 4 reached the semifinals
- 2 reached the finals

And when I was holding the cup in my hand, I never asked God:
"Why me?"

Sometimes, you are not satisfied with your life but remember that many people in this world are dreaming of living your life.

Live simple, be happy! Walk humbly and love genuinely.

My recommendation is not to read this book just once. It is a framework to design your LIFE, so read it again, until you get your framework in place. Start early and be your own BEST.

For comments and sharing your experience do drop a note on…

 www.Pride-Thebook.com

 @pridebegin   @pridebegin

Allow your **PASSION**
To become your
PURPOSE,
And it will one day become your
PROFESSION.

- Gabrielle Bernstein

Made in United States
Orlando, FL
22 March 2026

79559017R00090